About Island Press

Since 1984, the nonprofit Island Press has been stimulating, shaping, and communicating the ideas that are essential for solving environmental problems worldwide. With more than 800 titles in print and some 40 new releases each year, we are the nation's leading publisher on environmental issues. We identify innovative thinkers and emerging trends in the environmental field. We work with world-renowned experts and authors to develop cross-disciplinary solutions to environmental challenges.

Island Press designs and implements coordinated book publication campaigns in order to communicate our critical messages in print, in person, and online using the latest technologies, programs, and the media. Our goal: to reach targeted audiences—scientists, policymakers, environmental advocates, the media, and concerned citizens—who can and will take action to protect the plants and animals that enrich our world, the ecosystems we need to survive, the water we drink, and the air we breathe.

Island Press gratefully acknowledges the support of its work by the Agua Fund, Inc., The Margaret A. Cargill Foundation, Betsy and Jesse Fink Foundation, The William and Flora Hewlett Foundation, The Kresge Foundation, The Forrest and Frances Lattner Foundation, The Andrew W. Mellon Foundation, The Curtis and Edith Munson Foundation, The Overbrook Foundation, The David and Lucile Packard Foundation, The Summit Foundation, Trust for Architectural Easements, The Winslow Foundation, and other generous donors.

The opinions expressed in this book are those of the author(s) and do not necessarily reflect the views of our donors.

GOOD URBANISM

Six Steps
to Creating
Prosperous
Places

NAN ELLIN

◑ **ISLAND**PRESS Washington | Covelo | London

Metropolitan Planning + Design
Series editors: Arthur C. Nelson and Reid Ewing

A collaboration between Island Press and the University of Utah's Department of City & Metropolitan Planning, this series provides a set of tools for students and professionals working to make our cities and metropolitan areas more sustainable, livable, prosperous, resilient, and equitable. As the world's population grows to nine billion by mid-century, the population of the US will rise to one-half billion. Along the way, the physical landscape will be transformed. Indeed, two-thirds of the built environment in the US at mid-century will be constructed between now and then, presenting a monumental opportunity to reshape the places we live. The *Metropolitan Planning + Design* series presents an integrated approach to addressing this challenge, involving the fields of planning, architecture, landscape architecture, urban design, public policy, environmental studies, geography, and civil and environmental engineering. The series draws from the expertise of some of the world's leading scholars in the field of Metropolitan Planning + Design. Please see Islandpress .org/Utah/ for more information.

Other books in the series:

The TDR Handbook, Arthur C. Nelson, Rick Pruetz, and Doug Woodruff (2011)
Stewardship of the Built Environment, Robert Young (2012)
Governance and Equity, Marc Brenman and Thomas W. Sanchez (2012)

Forthcoming:
Reshaping Metropolitan America, Arthur C. Nelson

Library of Congress Cataloging-in-Publication Data

Ellin, Nan.
 Good urbansim : six steps to creating prosperous places / Nan Ellin.
   p. cm. — (Metropolitan planning + design)
 Includes bibliographical references and index.
 ISBN 978-1-61091-364-5 (cloth : alk. paper) — ISBN 1-61091-364-7 (cloth : alk. paper) —
 ISBN 978-1-61091-374-4 (pbk. : alk. paper) — ISBN 1-61091-374-4 (pbk. : alk. paper) 1.
City planning. 2. Community development, Urban. I. Title.
 HT166.E45 2012
 307.1'216—dc23   2012022388

Printed using Minion

Text design by Maureen Gately
Typesetting by Sztrecska Publishing

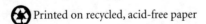Printed on recycled, acid-free paper

Manufactured in the United States of America
10 9 8 7 6 5 4 3 2 1

Keywords: BIMStorm and Onuma System, Canalscape, Cedar Approach, Civic Center,
community design, ecosystems, Envision Utah, Groundwork, the High Line, integral
urbanism, Open Space Seattle 2100, polish, present, promote, propose, prospect,
prototype, public art, Sunrise Park, University of Arkansas Community
Design Center, urban design, urban planning

To my parents,
   Carole & Morty

Contents

Acknowledgments

FIRST AND FOREMOST, I WISH TO THANK BRENDA SCHEER for helping me find the spark of this book, fostering a rich and welcoming environment in the College of Architecture + Planning at the University of Utah, and bringing me to this very special place. I also want to recognize my colleagues in the Planning Department, who are as gracious as they are gifted: Keith Bartholomew, Philip Emmi, Reid Ewing, Stephen Goldsmith, Michael Larice, Arthur C. Nelson, Tariq Banuri, and Pamela Perlich. For taking care of us all, I am very grateful to Jeannette Benson.

I have had the good fortune of encountering just the right guides along the path of writing this book. On a hilltop of Rome, I met psychologist James Hillman, whose insights helped navigate the course, particularly those about restoring soul to the places we live, the transformative power of the image, and the need to be "rooted in the earth" in order to grow. Also in Rome, sociologist Zygmunt Bauman offered timely feedback that provided essential intellectual and creative sustenance. The work of Peter Block, Otto Scharmer, and Charlene Spretnak helped steer me through some challenging terrain. I've been energized and inspired by exemplary practices of colleagues around the globe, many of whom are profiled here.

My earlier teachers at Bryn Mawr College, at Columbia University, and during my Fulbright year in France illuminated the way forward by modeling a dedication to their craft, most notably Judith Shapiro, Robert Murphy, Peter Marcuse, Saskia Sassen, Herbert Gans, Kenneth Jackson, Kenneth Frampton, Mary McLeod, Richard Plunz, Barry Bergdoll, Nicole and Antoine Haumont, and Françoise Choay. For guidance throughout the journey, I humbly express my gratitude to Jane Jacobs, a beacon whose enduring and widespread impact is testament to the value of her work and wisdom.

Some of my greatest teachers have been my students, especially Samuel Feldman, Braden Kay, Rose Kane, Michael McDearmon, and Yuri Artibise. For challenging and enlightening me, I thank them as well as other members of the Canalscape team: David Proffitt, Stephen Buckman, Dan Bartman, Andrea Baty, Francisco Cardona, Antonio Molina, Paul Iverson, Charlie Jannetto, Jill Johnson, David Crummey, Keith Mulvin, Christopher Kuzdas, Brynn Martin, Bernardo Marquez, Allison Segal, Riley Smith, Peter St. Andrews, Robin Stamp, and Constance Taylor. My dear friend Ellen Macks ignited the Canalscape flame with her insight and encouragement. This flame has been kept alive thanks to generous support from the Arizona Humanities Council, SRP, Jay Hicks, Mark Stapp, Diane Brossart, Bruce Hallin, and James Duncan.

For assistance with the case studies in this book, I thank Jennifer J. Johnson, Justinian Popa, Elizabeth Gray, and Joshua Edward. For creating the diagrams, I thank Trent Smith, Elizabeth Gray, Amir Hajrasouliha, and Kaitlin Barklow. Chad Atterbury of AECOM provided the cover image depicting canalscape. I am grateful to Andrea Garfinkel-Castro, Keri Williams, Sara Meess, and Amir Hajrasouliha, who offered valuable feedback on an early draft. I am extremely appreciative of Heather Boyer for her keen sense and sensibility. It has been a privilege and pleasure to work with her and others from Island Press.

An Honors Professorship Award from the Honors College at the University of Utah has allowed me to share the Path toward Prosperity with students through the Salt Lake City Workshop (http://slcworkshop.org). I thank Martha Bradley for providing this opportunity and acknowledge the first students in the workshop who helped bring the Nine Line to Salt Lake City: Nate Currey, Sean Morgan, Joseph Briggs, Solomon Carter, Molly Clark, Austin Dent, Dustin Fratto, Johanna Jamison, Annika Jones, Shannon Miller, and Justinian Popa. I also wish to thank our partners from the City of Salt Lake with whom we worked to link neighborhoods and bring an abandoned rail corridor back to life, particularly Frank Gray, Mary DeLaMare-Schaefer, Bob Farrington, Cheri Coffey, Dan Velasquez, Timothy Harpst, Elizabeth Reining, Nick Britton, and Jessica Thesing. I extend a special thanks to Mayor (and planner) Ralph Becker for his ongoing engagement with our planning department and for cohosting the annual Mayor's Symposium.

Everything I know about community I learned from my parents, Carole and Morty Ellin—and their one hundred best friends—while growing up in Baltimore. This book is dedicated to them with love and gratitude for encouraging me to find my own path and for their unwavering support along the way. As my daughter, Theodora, embarks for college, I dearly wish her the same and send her off with admiration, appreciation, and *bon courage* from the heart. For accompanying me on this path, I am ever grateful to Dan Hoffman—my architect, favorite DJ, twin flame, and co-creator in life.

Nan Ellin
Salt Lake City, August 2011

1 | Introduction

A HOUSE I ONCE LIVED IN CAME WITH A POTTED GRAPE IVY. I watered the plant regularly, but oddly, it never grew. It didn't die, but during the two years I lived there, it never changed shape or sprouted a leaf. Leaving this grape ivy behind for the next inhabitants, it became emblematic for me of so many places that, while they may be surviving, are clearly not thriving.

For most of human history, we built habitats that supported us more than they challenged us. As industrialization began shifting the scale and logic of urbanization, however, we veered off course and became the only species to build habitats that are not sustainable. Over the last several decades, we have been making concerted efforts to get back on course and construct places that support humanity more optimally, places that sustain us rather than strain us.

Thanks to these efforts, *there is now a virtual consensus among planners and urban designers about what constitutes good urbanism.*[1] This consensus holds that networks of quality public spaces should be lined with and punctuated by vital hubs of activity. Stated inversely, urban regions should be comprised of mixed-use cores (large hubs and smaller nodes) connected by corridors of transit, automobile, and bicycle routes as well as other quality public spaces to ensure walkability.[2] These public spaces include outdoor places—for circulation, recreation, and preservation of natural landscapes—as well as indoor cultural institutions and gathering places.[3] Good urbanism honors the past by preserving historic fabrics and adaptively reusing existing structures. It also honors the future by celebrating creativity through supporting new and innovative architecture, public art, and entrepreneurship at all scales. Good urbanism offers a full spectrum of housing options, accommodating a wide range of household types and income levels, comprising a diverse community that is actively engaged in shaping and managing its future.

Key to good urbanism is the connective tissue: infrastructure, public space, and community engagement. Whether retrofitted or new, for practical purposes or pleasure, infrastructure is integrated with public spaces and both are multipurpose, technologically advanced, attractive, and harmonious with natural and cultural settings.[4] Community-building and engagement occur spontaneously in the quality public space as well as more deliberatively through interesting and fun initiatives sponsored by municipal organizations, community groups, or businesses.[5] In sum, good urbanism is vital, vibrant, safe, comfortable, legible, accessible, equitable, efficient, elegant, convenient, walkable, sustainable, beautiful, distinctive, and dynamic.[6]

While there are numerous iterations with a range of foci, most recommendations converge on these principles. Along with this knowledge of the component parts of good urbanism, we also have the will, the tools, and the resources to achieve these desired ends. Nevertheless, their actual delivery remains challenging and all too rare. Good urbanism still eludes in far too many instances; hence the continued proliferation of prescriptions for healing ailing places.

We know where we want to go, but cannot reliably get there. Why not?[7] With the intensified division of labor regarding the built environment over the last century, it can be difficult to identify the sources of dissatisfaction with our places and thereby address them. For example, in search of authenticity and identity, jurisdictions and institutions sometimes turn to branders, usually from another city or even another country, who ironically tend to stamp similar marks of "identity" (brands) wherever they go. In search of distinction and status, "starchitects" may be commissioned who typically have priorities other than serving the greater good. In search of vitality, made-to-order "lifestyle centers" are dropped onto greenfield sites. Stakeholder meetings are convened to obtain buy-in, rather than feedback. And so on.

Having lost our compass, the quest to improve places for all people is too often estranged from the places and communities themselves. Consequently, an untold number of excellent proposals are never realized or unfortunately compromised, while many suboptimal ones are implemented. As a result, valuable resources (human, economic, political, and environmental) are squandered as our towns, cities, and regions suffer the consequences.

We have, to some extent, buried our instinctual capacity to create habitats that support us most fully, places where we may thrive. This book asks what exactly has been lost and describes a path for uncovering this buried urban instinct, dusting it off, and updating it to serve us today.[8]

Anyone can walk this path, professionals in the field of urbanism—planners, urban designers, architects, or landscape architects—and others alike. The only precondition for stepping onto the path is a willingness to let it take us someplace we've never been before. In other words, a prerequisite for good urbanism is knowing what (or that) we don't know. The job of the professional urbanist includes directing people toward the path and providing some assistance along the way.

The next chapter, "Urban Desiderata" (chapter 2), clears the way toward this new territory by describing six steps along the path to better places. Chapter 3, "The Tao of Urbanism," explains how this path renders the latent manifest and the possible inevitable by building on personal and collective assets to build on the strengths of places. The fourth chapter, "Co-Creation," delves more deeply into collective and place prospecting. "Going with the Flow" (chapter 5) describes how to polish the gemstones mined during personal, collective, and place prospecting and how to craft transformative place proposals through urban acupuncture, the five qualities of integral urbanism, and learning from ecosystems.

Chapter 6, "The Art of Urbanism," offers a handy guide for following the six steps along the path, as well as recommendations for effectively communicating place proposals and recovering our urban instinct. The seventh chapter, "From Good to Great Urbanism," limns the contours of an emergent paradigm, moving beyond sustainability to prosperity. "Sideways Urbanism" (chapter 8) demonstrates how this new paradigm operates in a way that is neither top-down nor bottom-up, but sideways. The concluding section (chapter 9) provides an overview of what it takes to be a good urbanist.

Case studies at the end of chapters 3 through 6, primarily from the United States, illustrate various aspects of good urbanism in practice. Learning from these examples and others, this book sets forth a process for imagining best possibilities and realizing them, with suggestions for navigating potential blind spots and potholes along the way. It instructs, incites, and inspires all to enhance the health and well-being of places and communities. It also contributes to the efficacy and relevance of the professions dedicated to these goals by adding a few essential items to the planning and urban design toolkits.

The pair of eyes in the "Good Urbanism" artwork evokes the two types of vision that are key to this approach: seeing the present and past clearly while envisioning better futures. The wink is a reminder to planners, urban designers, architects, and landscape architects that good urbanism is the goal of our endeavors, not joining or starting a camp and competing against others for supremacy. The wink also refers to the *ensō* embedded in "Good," a Japanese symbol for strength and elegance. In Zen Buddhism, the ensō expresses the moment when the mind is free to let the body and spirit create, an opening that reveals a connection with something larger and an opportunity to participate in the co-creation of an always incomplete and imperfect world. The child-like rendering of the Good conveys the inherent simplicity and authenticity of this approach.

2 | Urban Desiderata: A Path toward Prosperity

WE USE STRONG WORDS WHEN WE TALK ABOUT PLACES, proclaiming our "love" or "hate" for a city, neighborhood, house, or other building. Indeed, we probably use these words more often with regard to place than people. Needless to say, the places we love support us, while the places we hate strain us.

What moves us to proclaim our "love" for a place?[1] Usually, we feel connected when we're there. We may feel connected to ourselves, others, the place itself, nature, a higher being, the past, or the future. When we realize these bonds, we feel a sense of meaning, harmony, purpose, interest, excitement, distinction, dynamism, safety, security, civility, mutual respect, and/or generosity of spirit. We often describe these places as "authentic" or "genuine." The less we feel connected in a place, the less we tend to like it.

Good urbanism fosters these connections in order to make places livable and lovable.[2] We do not need more prescription lists or manifestos about what constitutes a good place. We need the ability to envision and manifest better possibilities for specific places that allow us to realize these bonds. How can we recapture this capacity to *cultivate good ideas for making livable and lovable places while rallying the resources to realize them*?

Learning from exemplary practices and applying insights from organizational learning, psychology, the philosophy of pragmatism, grounded theory, and wisdom traditions, I've developed an approach for uncovering the urban instinct to enhance human habitats. This "Path toward Prosperity" consists of six steps: prospect, polish, propose, prototype, promote, and present (figure 2.1, plate 1).

The first step along the path is excavation to **prospect** for buried gems. Prospecting involves listening to self, others, and places. Listening to self, or *personal prospecting*, begins with self-reflection about a particular project and the expression of initial ideas in words and images.[3] This step recognizes important hunches that might otherwise be overlooked, honoring our individual perspectives and intuitions and helping us understand any biases and motivations.[4] Personal prospecting is also essential because, unrecognized, this inner voice may become so loud it is impossible to hear anything else, including the voices of others and significant research findings. Even with the best intentions, it can be difficult to engage others without trying to control the outcome.

Just as flight attendants advise us to secure our own oxygen masks before assisting others, it is important we listen to ourselves so we can be receptive to others. It also helps to recognize and build on our own strengths in order to help others build on theirs. To breathe life into our places, we must first breathe well ourselves.

Once personal gems are revealed, the next step is *collective prospecting*, which involves sharing our gems with others and learning about their gems.[5] At the same time, *place prospecting* begins, the extracting of gems from specific locales through observation and effective community engagement. Then, research is undertaken into relevant history, political and economic conditions, best practices, site conditions, and so forth. All three kinds of prospecting contribute to **polishing** the gems (figure 2.2).

The third step is envisioning best possibilities and **proposing** plans, policies, and designs for crafting the polished nuggets into jewels that add economic, social, aesthetic, and environmental value to places. At this point, the proposal may be **prototyped** for testing and additional feedback. Then, the concept is **promoted** to a larger public to obtain even more input and build support. Well taken, these steps generate the resources required to implement the project along the way.

Ultimately, the project is **presented** to trustworthy partners capable of realizing the vision on an ongoing basis, and the initial catalyst may move on

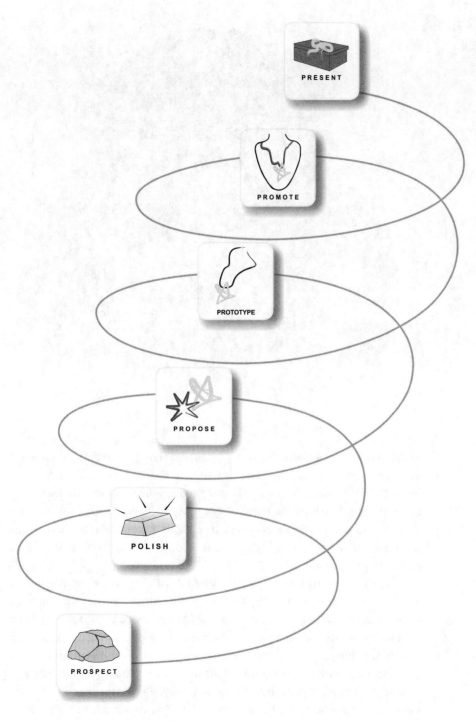

Figure 2.1 Path toward Prosperity: Prospect → Polish → Propose → Prototype → Promote → Present

Figure 2.2 Three kinds of prospecting

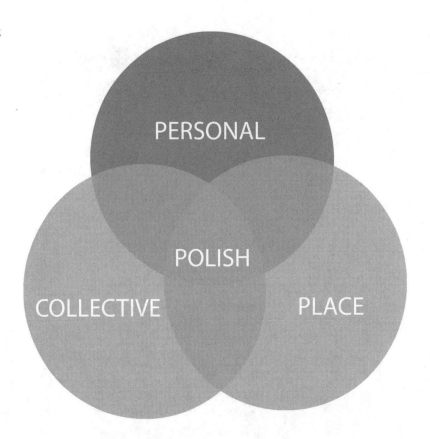

to catalyze other projects. Neither mountains (large interventions imposed deductively on a place) nor pebbles strewn about (too small to have an impact), these jewels are graciously endowed to adorn and enrich places and communities. Pursuing the path toward prosperity ignites sparks of creativity that animate places so they ring true to all, become the pride of communities who maintain and adapt them accordingly over time, and have an enduring positive impact.

The Path toward Prosperity offers a tool for *designing the process* to be adjusted on a case-by-case basis. For an initiative already at the proposal stage or beyond, but stalling, it may make sense to dip down and prospect in order to spiral back up and reenergize the project. In some instances, promoting may begin during the collective prospecting in the form of an ideas competition, or prototyping may not occur until after promoting. Projects will accord varying emphases to different steps along the path. In sum, the six steps are a heuristic device to be calibrated and customized for each project.

Box 2.1 Six Steps to Creating Prosperous Places

The Path toward Prosperity is a tool for *designing the process,* calibrated to each instance. The only requisite for stepping onto this path is a willingness to learn from self, others, and places. At each of the six steps along the way, we ask questions.

PROSPECT

Prospect

1. *Personal Prospecting* — What do I see, hear, smell, taste, feel, remember, and imagine in this place? What do I think should happen here?

2. *Collective Prospecting* — Ask others: What do you love/value about this place? How would you like to see it evolve?

3. *Place Prospecting* — What are the relevant historical, geological, geographic, political, economic, and sociocultural aspects of this place?

POLISH

Polish

Bringing the three kinds of prospecting together, ask: What are the strengths of this place and how can I co-create with others to build on them?

PROPOSE

Propose

What do we want here and how are we going to make it happen? (Advancement of plans, designs, and policies.)

PROTOTYPE

Prototype

How can we demonstrate this proposal to share the concept more fully, and to test and refine it?

PROMOTE

Promote

What is the best way to communicate the proposal to a larger public and obtain additional feedback as well as support?

PRESENT

Present

Who has emerged as the most able entity to steward this project onward and how can we pass the baton to this entity successfully?

3 | The Tao of Urbanism: Rendering the Latent Manifest and the Possible Inevitable

That flowing imagination which founded the city in the first place can be re-found. It is planted in our midst always ready to flower—if we begin, not with the "problem" of what needs to be changed, or moved, or built, or demolished, but begin with what already is here, still stands and sings of its soul.
—James Hillman (2006, 18)

ARTISANS, ARTISTS, DESIGNERS, CHOREOGRAPHERS, and other creators shape their work from the resources at hand: materials, dancers, money, land, and other given resources. If they devoted their time and energy to bemoaning what they lacked, they would never bring anything of value forth into the world. In similar fashion, when we build on our own gifts, rather than dwell on inadequacies, our strengths grow stronger. Some Native Americans consider these intrinsic gifts our "original medicine," endowing unique personal power so we may serve the world most optimally.[1] The Taoist tradition, hailing from fifth century BCE China, maintains that awareness and trust of our own inner nature allow us to be our best and avoid manipulation by others. These and other wisdom traditions exhort us to honor this rich source of authenticity and creativity.

Likewise, when we identify the assets of places, the *data* (given, or gifts), these too may flourish. When considering how best to improve the places we live, then, what if we focus on what we value rather than on what we can't stand? What if we devote special attention to what works rather than lament what doesn't? What if we recognize all we appreciate, cultivating gratitude in the process? The goal would not be faultfinding, but gift finding. Truffle-sniffing pigs, unearthing delicacies for all to enjoy.

In most instances, problems are what propel us to address issues and make changes. Rather than beeline directly to resolve the problems, the path toward prosperity resists this temptation and begins instead with a step aside, enlarging the perspective and gathering the gifts. It was this step aside that enabled the conversion of an abandoned elevated railway, regarded widely as a liability, into an outstanding amenity for New York City (see the High Line case study later in this chapter). In the Phoenix region, it generated a proposal for leveraging an extensive canal infrastructure into a distributed system of vital urban hubs along the water (see the Canalscape case study later in this chapter). Building on existing assets in a former brownfield in Minneapolis, what could have been an isolated ballpark became an urban neighborhood combining entertainment, transit, and clean energy generation (see the Groundwork case study in chapter 6).

During this personal, collective, and place prospecting, including "hope stories" (Kretzmann and McKnight 1993) for the future, we may also turn attention to past missteps and current obstacles along with "the powerful emotions that underpin many planning issues" (Sandercock 2003, 163). Since our survival imperative naturally scans the horizon for potential threats to our well-being, it is important these are voiced. Airing these issues freely in the company of others can help address the threats effectively, dissipate contempt, enable forgiveness of wrongdoing, and allow grieving of irrevocable losses. Collective prospecting can also help us avoid repeating previous missteps, strengthen resolve to make improvements, and even transform our greatest problems into our greatest solutions.

Raising these concerns is essential, but once they have been sufficiently addressed, it is equally important to shift attention back to what we value and what we want. Dwelling on needs and lacks ultimately corrodes hope, confidence, and will, rendering people demoralized and helpless. It can generate anxiety leading to fear and denial along with a scarcity mentality that spurs unhealthy competition, suppresses creative problem solving, and may prove paralyzing.[2] It can devolve into finger-pointing and ascribing blame, leading to partisan bickering with the goal of triumphing over others, rather than assuming responsibility for the problems we perceive. While ascribing blame may satisfy a need to exonerate oneself from wrongdoing or having to take action, it also disempowers those who point the finger and engenders power struggles instead of proaction. This clearly works against a robust discussion where past hurts and present differences are discussed openly, without fear of exclusion or retribution. Dwelling on needs and lacks, and their attendant behaviors, is not the path toward reaching a better outcome for all involved, toward nurturing and supporting life.

Conversely, focusing on strengths shifts the momentum toward spiraling up, instead of down. Our collective "original medicine" contributes to healing places, similar to "salutogenesis," an approach to healing people that "focuses on factors that support human health and well-being rather than on factors that cause disease" (Scharmer 2007, 469). Valuing what exists is ultimately empowering, while solely lamenting deficiencies undermines. Hence, though "critical thinking" is an important skill, it should always be accompanied by "appreciative thinking."[3] Critical thinking is best applied toward proaction, rather than an end in itself. Once the focus shifts to identifying gifts, these gifts tend to multiply.

In sum, focusing attention on what we lack or don't want only exacerbates the problem or pushes it elsewhere, eroding prosperity instead of building it. For instance, if a conversation begins with a discussion about lack of safety and security, the solution may be gates, which ignite more fear, more fortressing, and so on. Alternatively, when the focus is on what is valued, we can build on these strengths and spiral up. In the case of safety and security, when the conversation shifts to the assets of people and place, dangers arise less frequently because of the relationships developed, and when they do arise, the solution may be block watches, community policing, or forms of natural surveillance such as Jane Jacobs's "eyes on the street," which she describes as "an intricate, almost unconscious, network of voluntary controls and standards among the people themselves, and enforced by the people themselves" (Jacobs 1961, 40).

When **prospecting** for collective and place gems, we can discover a community's values by mining what anthropologist Clifford Geertz calls "local knowledge" (Geertz 1995). This is accomplished simply by consulting the "local experts," those who live and work in a place. In the case of architects working with clients, Norman Weinstein (2009a) advises: "Persuasion is always a major component of architectural communication—but begin with the invitation a door proposes," inviting clients in to openly communicate their needs and desires. Working at the scale of neighborhoods or cities, collective and place prospecting begins from the ground up, revealing the local gifts to discover an expanded field of *genius loci*, the "spirit of a place" recognized since ancient times as much more than its physical manifestation (Norberg-Schulz 1980).

Once these gems coalesce, we can **polish** them and craft **proposals** that are unique and appropriate to each situation. As Jaime Lerner, former mayor of Curitiba, Brazil, asserts, "Every great city has a vocation" (in ReGenesis and Taller 13 2009). Urban design teams ReGenesis and Taller 13 (2009) explain: "A vocation is the important work that a community is being called to do to serve something larger than itself. It is what a community is becoming, and always involves a stretch beyond what it currently is able to do." Collective and place prospecting reveals this important work, unlocking the potential of communities.[4]

To discover a place's vocation and craft these proposals, good urbanism identifies the local strengths and ensures their preservation. These strengths may include natural landscapes, buildings, monuments, public art, neighborhoods, businesses, cultural institutions, and human attributes and talents. Recognizing existing assets and capacities inflects the process, invariably leading to a consideration of what could be improved with minor adjustments. Only after identifying and protecting what is valued, and enhancing what may be underperforming, do we address what is missing and should be added. Good urbanism preserves buildings, neighborhoods, and natural landscapes that are valued; reclaims, rehabilitates, restores, or renovates what is underperforming; and then adds new elements—all informed by effective community involvement. A helpful mnemonic for this approach is PEA: Protect, Enhance, and Add (figure 3.1).

Figure 3.1 PEA: Protect, Enhance, and Add

Too often, urban interventions proceed in the reverse order, considering first what needs to be added. Over the last century, many urban design projects have even opted to begin with a *tabula rasa*, a blank (or, more precisely, "erased") slate, privileging pristine land upon which to erect master plans or razing what was already there. While that approach may succeed in adding the new requested elements, it often does so at the expense of what was valued.[5]

Rather than neglect, abandon, or erase our urban heritage, good urbanism is inspired by what is integral to a place—its DNA—and builds upon these assets.[6] Beginning with a *tabula plena*, or full slate, this process allows unique and meaningful expressions to unfold because when people are invited to share what they value, they become empowered and creative. At the same time, this process builds trust and mutual respect, allowing a range of stakeholders to learn and evolve along with the facilitators, co-creating proposals that are neither divisive nor lowest common denominators, but larger than the sum of their individual parts. By enlisting a wide array of invested parties, support and resources come forth to realize visions, and the basis for an ongoing self-adjusting feedback mechanism is established.[7]

The PEA process also addresses what is lacking, along with issues from the past, but since these are no longer the point of departure, when they arise they become opportunities. Describing this process as "creative planning," Charles Landry, prime mover of the Creative City movement, explains that it "is based on the idea of cultural resources and the holistic notion that every problem is merely an opportunity in disguise; every weakness has a potential strength and that even the seemingly 'invisible' can be made into something positive" (Landry 2006, 10–11).

Hence, this process finds valuable kernels in perceived challenges. For instance, a graffiti "problem" could engage youth in creating ever-changing "art walls" that grace the city, converting "vandals" into budding artists recognized for their work that is beautifying the city.[8] Urban "blight" can be converted into partially inhabited and evocatively placemaking "ruins."[9] Abandonment of downtown cores leaving many vacant lots can yield to productive landscapes.[10] Foreclosed properties (redfields) can become greenfields. Stormwater can be converted into greenfrastructure (see the University of Arkansas Community Design Center case study in chapter 5). A desert city's "problem" of too much sun could be its opportunity to become a global leader in solar energy. Or, a region's "problem" of low water supply could be an opportunity to demonstrate innovative water management strategies, updating the tradition of its ancient ancestors. Instead of being regarded as "social issues," differences among people can be celebrated as opportunities for learning, innovation, and creative entrepreneurship. Performing urban alchemy, we collectively transmute this *prima materia* into the gold discovered on the path toward prosperity.

Considering urban design practices specifically, architect Mohsen Mostafavi (2010, 3) advocates such an approach: "We need to view the fragility of the planet and its resources as an opportunity for speculative design innovations. . . . By extension, the problems confronting our cities and regions would then become opportunities to define a new approach. Imagining an urbanism that is other than the status quo requires a new sensibility." Also expressing this attitude, architect and planner Brenda Scheer (2010, 112) asserts: "Imagination is key. . . . Perhaps this is the most important role for urban design—not so much to tear down and build anew but to offer a different view of the future based on what is already happening."

California firm Bunch Design evocatively demonstrates the *tabula plena* sensibility with their proposition for Tree People (figure 3.2). Reversing standard development practices, this provocation inserts human habitats into existing nature, so that development does not follow "the rule of an engineer's curb but rather the guidance of the land" (Sundius and Ichiki 2011).

Figure 3.2 Tree People by Bunch Design (Credit: Sundius and Ichiki)

Focusing on possibilities, rather than problems, reduces the tendency to dwell on past mistakes and resent past wrongs and instead redirects energy that would be devoted to lamenting, whining, complaining, or parrying to positively influencing the future. Beginning with gifts, rather than deficits, inspires capacity building and builds confidence and morale in individuals as well as groups, spilling over into other arenas. A perception of scarcity is supplanted by one of abundance, converting a zero-sum economy into a limitless one, and turning competition into fruitful collaboration.[11] In the process, what may have been perceived as the greatest problems or weaknesses become the greatest strengths, and the virtuous cycle—or spiral—replaces the vicious one. Robert Kennedy famously evoked this attitude when he said, "There are those who look at things the way they are, and ask why. . . . I dream of things that never were, and ask why not?"[12]

In community development, John Kretzman and John McKnight call this approach Asset-Based Community Development (ABCD), which they describe as follows: "The key to neighborhood regeneration . . . is to locate all of the available local assets, to begin connecting them with one another in ways that multiply their power and effectiveness, and to begin harnessing those local institutions that are not yet available for local development purposes" (Kretzmann and McKnight 1993). To assist this kind of community building, the popular SWOT (Strengths, Weaknesses, Opportunities, and Threats) analysis may be replaced by a SOAR (Strengths, Opportunities, Aspirations, and Results) analysis (Stavros and Hinrichs 2009).

C. Otto Scharmer and Peter Block, leaders in the field of organizational learning and change, similarly emphasize the importance of shifting from problems to possibilities and from focusing on the past to focusing on the future. Scharmer (2007) maintains that problem solving is about making improvements on the past, while possibility finding focuses on the future. Likewise, Block (2008, 29) writes: "The context that restores community is one of possibility, generosity, and gifts, rather than one of problem solving, fear, and retribution. A new context acknowledges that we have all the capacity, expertise, and resources that an alternative future requires. Communities are human systems given form by conversations that build relatedness. . . . Conversations that focus on stories about the past become a limitation to the community; ones that are teaching parables and focus on the future restore community." We create the new context, Block maintains, by shifting from blaming others to taking responsibility, from retributive to restorative practices.

Adopting restorative practices, good urbanism could also take cues from restorative justice, a movement that has proven successful around the globe over the past few decades. Rather than punish criminal offenders, restorative justice focuses on repairing harm done to people and relationships. Restorative justice moves beyond the conventional punitive–permissive continuum, inserting it within a larger matrix along the axes of support and control, adding neglectful as well as restorative approaches (see figure 3.3). The restorative approach employs high control over wrongdoing while supporting and valuing the intrinsic worth of the wrongdoer. In a similar spirit, good urbanism applies capacity building to the restoration of places.

The language of restoration and prosperity is spoken widely by environmentalists. Paul Hawken, environmentalist and entrepreneur, called for a shift to prosperity through a "restoration economy" in 1993. A restoration economy, he explained, builds on and works with ecosystems, restor-

Figure 3.3 Restorative justice matrix: Good urbanism values the intrinsic worth of places as restorative justice values the intrinsic worth of people (Credit: Adapted from http://www.restorativepractices.org)

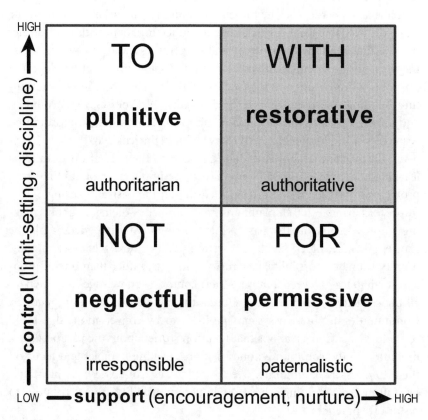

ing natural (including human) capital as a vital economic foundation and shifting investment decisions from short-term returns to longer-term returns that include costs of natural resources, unemployment, health issues, and so forth. Hawken maintains: "Humans want to flourish and prosper . . . and they will eventually reject any system of conservation that interferes with these desires. [Prosperity] will only come about through the accumulated effects of daily acts of billions of eager participants" (1993, xv).[13] Environmentalist Bill McKibben similarly advocates a shift from "growth" as the paramount economic ideal to the pursuit of prosperity, accomplished through localism: places producing more of their own energy, food, and local culture and entertainment. By nurturing the essential humanity of our economy, he contends, we recapture our own humanity (McKibben 2007, 17).

To help make places more "lovable"—so people will feel more connected and supported—good urbanists reframe the initial question from "What is the problem?" to "What are the strengths of the place and how can we build on these?" Rather than ask "What *don't* you want?", good urbanists listen attentively to how people answer the question "What *do* you want?" The value-free objective expert becomes a receptive participant-observer learning about local knowledge and building trust (relationships) through honesty and authenticity. The remote, white-jacketed scientist peering down from on high steps down to engage communities, cultivating mutual respect in the process. Moving beyond ascribing blame to taking responsibility, from re-acting to pro-acting, good urbanists practice leadership as the art of gathering people and ideas to make a difference through pursuing the path toward prosperity.[14]

In sum, good urbanism makes the latent manifest by building on our own strengths in order to build on the strengths of places. It also renders the possible, and sometimes even the improbable, inevitable by generating support along the way, thereby rallying resources to realize the vision. Good urbanism is highly inductive, taking cues from the data (or gifts), connecting the dots among these assets, and adding value to them through collective envisioning to effect significant and ongoing change, the focus of the next chapter.

PROJECT: The High Line

LOCATION: New York City, NY

KEY PLAYERS: Joshua David, Robert Hammond, Casey Jones, James Corner Field Operations, Diller Scofidio + Renfro, Piet Oudolf, Friends of the High Line, City of New York

MAJOR THEMES: Flow; local; nature in the city; connected open space systems; adaptive infrastructure reuse; walkability; entrepreneurial creativity; collaborative teams; co-creation with stakeholders; community engagement; conversations about urbanism

> "The bottom line is that the High Line will have to come down."
> —*New York City planning commissioner Joseph Rose (quoted in Lueck, 1999)*

CASE STUDY WRITTEN BY JENNIFER J. JOHNSON WITH NAN ELLIN

Joshua David and Robert Hammond first met in the summer of 1999 at a community board meeting to discuss the future of the High Line. Originally built in the 1930s as an elevated railway thirty feet above ground along the lower west side of Manhattan, the High Line had been abandoned since the 1980s. At the time of this meeting, Mayor Giuliani and many others regarded the High Line as a liability for the neighborhoods it traversed and were working to have it demolished. The meeting room was filled with property owners and developers, some of whom had spent two decades fighting in and out of court to bring about the demise of the "blighted" and "hazardous" rail (David 2002, 14). One developer in particular spent $3 million himself opposing anything but demolition (C. Jones 2011).

David and Hammond, however, regarded the High Line as "an irreplaceable piece of New York City infrastructure" that could be transformed into an amenity for the entire city (David 2002, 17), offering a linear park with magnificent views of the Hudson River and the New York skyline. Thanks to their vision and perseverance, the High Line has become "this generation's Central Park," according to former city councilman Gifford Miller (Friends of the High Line 2005), with fifty thousand people using it on nice days (Hiller 2011).

Hammond is a second-generation friend of parks (his father founded San Antonio's Friends of the Parks organization) with a degree in history from Princeton (Hiller 2011). The self-taught painter, Internet startup veteran, and arts organizer considers the High Line a "place where his creativity and love of

PROSPECT

'starting things' collide" (Hiller 2011). "I was most interested in the underside—the steel and girders," Hammond recalls. "Then I saw the top—a mile and a half of wildflowers. I loved this juxtaposition—the hard and soft, the tame and wild. I really became interested in preserving it, but keeping it wide open" (Hammond 2011). David, a freelance writer for *Fortune*, *Gourmet*, *Travel + Leisure*, and other publications, was smitten by its linear quality. "No other open space or transportation corridor in the five boroughs allows a pedestrian to walk 22 blocks without crossing a single street, to pass through city blocks, to view from a floating vantage point the Hudson River, midtown skyscrapers, and the muscular industrial architecture of the lower west side" (David 2002, 18).

Pairing their personal visions for the High Line, the two commenced collective and place prospecting. Hammond's parents introduced them to Elizabeth Barlow Rogers, founder of the Central Park Conservancy, and Warrie Price, executive director of the Battery Park Conservancy (Hiller 2011), who provided critical insight into realizing such an ambitious project as well as the credibility to engage significant stakeholders. Rogers penned an article to lend legitimacy to the project, and Price visited the Promenade Plantée in Paris, an inspiration to the High Line, so she could testify before the New York City Council in support of the proposal (Hiller 2011). David researched the history and legal aspects of the High Line and, after "five years of fundraising, permit applications and even a lawsuit against the city" (National Public Radio 2011), eventually obtained the essential federal Certificate of Interim Trail Use, allowing the government to "rail-bank" the abandoned rail corridor as a trail in case the country may need it at a later point.

David and Hammond were awarded a grant from the Design Trust for Public Space, which allowed them to hire urbanist Casey Jones to assist in producing *Reclaiming the High Line*, "a study to examine the potential of this historic structure" (High Line 2011). In addition to the Promenade Plantée, Jones studied other precedents, such as the Stone Arch Bridge bikeway and pedestrian venue in Minneapolis. He also looked to New York City's own urban form for inspiration, analyzing Rockefeller Center and Lincoln Center and finding that a reinterpreted High Line would be akin to the namesake "park" of Park Avenue—"public space made possible by an underlying rail corridor" (David 2002, 19).

With Jones, David and Hammond inventoried the High Line's assets, including its unsurpassed location and the fact that it was already being used as a pedestrian site, either unauthorized or via a tangled permission process (David 2002, 81). They also had engineers ensure the rail's structural stability and investigated reuse laws and funding opportunities. To engage the larger community, they started the nonprofit Friends of the High Line, which grew rapidly to include a wide range of participants, from the arts community to professionals, neighbors,

POLISH

fashion designer Diane von Furstenberg, actor Edward Norton, the New York Jets football franchise, and the "Save Gansevoort Market" initiative, which was seeking to maintain the meat-packing district's historic designation. Friends of the High Line also found powerful advocates in politicians, from city council members to U.S. senator Hillary Rodham Clinton, U.S. senator Charles E. Schumer, and U.S. representative Jerrold Nadler, who helped secure essential city and federal funding.

To obtain support from property owners, Friends of the High Line worked with the New York City Council to enact a Transfer of Development Rights (TDR), allowing air rights to be transferred up and down the length of the line, providing strong incentives for property owners by increasing the potential square footage of projects (C. Jones 2011). They also produced "an economic feasibility study that showed the High Line would easily double its original $150 million cost in tax revenue from increased property values in the area. (That revenue figure has since been raised to nearly half a billion dollars)" (National Public Radio 2011). Friends of the High Line organized four advisory sessions with politicians, architects, and other experts to garner more information and a range of perspectives as well as support.

PROPOSE   **PROMOTE**

In 2003, Friends of the High Line launched the open ideas competition "Designing the High Line" (http://www.thehighline.org/competition/), which received over seven hundred entries from thirty-six countries. Several hundred were displayed at Grand Central Terminal, significantly broadening the conversation. As Jones explained: "A lot of the time, the public only sees a product when it's completed. . . .We frontloaded it instead. This allowed the public to share ideas of what something could become, not [just] what it was" (C. Jones 2011).

In 2004, Friends of the High Line partnered with the City of New York to launch a professional design competition. Seven teams were shortlisted, then narrowed down to four finalists. The team that was awarded the commission consisted of landscape architects James Corner Field Operations, architects Diller Scofidio + Renfro, and planting designer Piet Oudolf. Building on what was already there, they proposed a "wildscape" interspersed with seating, original rail tracks, and features that highlighted views and offered interesting moments along the linear park (figures 3.4 and 3.5, plates 5 and 6).

"Mayor Giuliani really wanted to demolish the High Line," Hammond (2011) says. "One of his last acts in office—two days before he left—was signing the demolition order." Support garnered by Friends of the High Line, however, prevented the demolition from taking place.

Figure 3.4 The High Line, designed by James Corner Field Operations, architects Diller Scofidio + Renfro, and planting designer Piet Oudolf (Credit: Master Gardeners of Mercer County)

Figure 3.5 Another view of the High Line (Credit: Master Gardeners of Mercer County)

PROTOTYPE

PRESENT

In 2005, the High Line south of 30th Street was donated to the City by CSX Transportation Inc., and ground was broken in 2006, with the first section opening in 2009, the second in 2011, and the third currently in progress and projected to be completed in 2014 (Pogrebin 2011). Responsibility for the park has been assumed by the New York City Department of Parks and Recreation, with maintenance provided by Friends of the High Line.

While the City of New York spent $115 million on the park, the project generated eight thousand construction jobs and a total of twelve thousand jobs in the area (McGeehan 2011). As a result, "what started out as a community-based campaign to convert an eyesore into an asset evolved into one of the most successful economic-development projects of the mayor's nine years in office" (McGeehan 2011).

Through this decade-long odyssey, Hammond and David presented New York City with "a glittering urban amenity" (Taylor 2010) and "the hippest public park this city has concocted" (Finn 2008). In Jones's estimation: "It's the creation of a new space and way of experiencing the city—the ability to be both the object, and in a sense a *voyeur*—[offering] interesting juxtapositions of private experiences in a very public, urban space" (C. Jones 2011). The High Line, Jones maintains, "was a beautiful pairing of the development of a social conduit . . . [and the] redevelopment of a neighborhood" (C. Jones 2011).

Inspiring "other people to start things" was one of Hammond's major goals for the project from the outset, helping them realize that "things don't always have to be top down" (Hammond 2011). He recounts: "We did not have a plan. We did not have the money. We did not even have a design—the things that people think you have to have when you start things. . . . People can help you with those things. It's really just getting it started and providing the rallying cry" (Hammond 2011).

PROJECT: Canalscape

LOCATION: Phoenix metropolitan region

KEY PLAYERS: Nan Ellin and the Canalscape Team

MAJOR THEMES: Flow; low; local; nature in the city; connected open space systems; network model for cities and regions; adaptive infrastructure reuse; canal-oriented development; walkability and bikeability; creative entrepreneurship; entrepreneurial creativity; collaborative teams; co-creation with stakeholders; community engagement; conversations about urbanism

Imagine going for a stroll or a jog along the canal. You're not dodging traffic, you're not hearing engines scream by and you're not sucking up vehicle exhaust. Instead, you're cruising along the waterway with other pedestrians, following the easy, quiet flow of the canal stream. Then you stumble upon a little marketplace. You can stop for coffee and read the paper, meet your friend for lunch or pop into a boutique for a little shopping.

Doesn't that sound like a dream?

It really doesn't have to be.

—*Lilia Menconi*

CASE STUDY WRITTEN BY JENNIFER J. JOHNSON

Blogger Lilia Menconi was referring to Canalscape, a proposal for making this dream a reality in the Phoenix metropolitan region. Introduced in 2009, Canalscape aims to catalyze "an authentic and sustainable desert urbanism" (Ellin 2009) for metropolitan Phoenix. Recognizing the region has more canal miles than Amsterdam and Venice combined, the Canalscape initiative aims to enhance quality of life and to reposition Phoenix as one of the world's great canal cities by creating vital urban hubs where canals meet major streets. From "the world's least sustainable city" (Ross 2011), Phoenix could become a city composed of livable and walkable neighborhoods, founded in history, and resilient into the future.

Over a millennium ago, the Hohokam Indian civilization built over six hundred miles of canals, with just their hands and stone hoes. This civilization disappeared from the region about five centuries ago, and white settlers discovered and reestablished the canal system in the late nineteenth century. Life revolved around the canals once again until the mid-twentieth century when air-conditioning, suburban tract development, infrastructure engineering, and lack of a sustainability ethic conspired to turn the canals from the front porches of the region to its back alleys (figure 3.6).

In an article written for the *Arizona Republic*, Ellin described her personal prospecting for this project as follows: "Leaving a mid-summer dry and dusty Phoenix, my daughter Theodora and I embarked for Paris several years ago to celebrate her 13th birthday. It was her first visit, but a return for me to a city where I had lived for two years, twenty years prior. This time around, I was struck by how deftly water features—both natural and constructed—weave through the Parisian urban fabric, creating a tapestry that appeals to eye and ear alike. This 'water tapestry'

PROSPECT

Figure 3.6 Post–World War II development turned its back to the canals (Credit: Nan Ellin)

also provides appealing places to gather with cool mists and pools for dangling feet, so welcome in the heat wave that had descended that year." Ellin realized that Phoenix also has a remarkable "water tapestry" in its canals that could be leveraged by developing vacant or underutilized parcels adjacent to the right-of-ways. Upon returning to Phoenix, she researched the numerous canal proposals over the decades, listened to people relate fond memories of swimming in and picnicking by the canals, and "began envisioning what it would mean to truly recognize, and build upon, this ancient gift of human ingenuity" (Ellin 2008).

In the article, Ellin enumerated the many benefits Canalscape would bring to the region. Enthusiastic response impelled her to launch the collective prospecting phase in a fashion to become the project's hallmark: multidisciplinary, community-driven, and ambitious. Twenty-two Arizona State University (ASU) students from ten different academic programs participated in the Canalscape Workshop, and fifteen additional students took part in a parallel urban design studio at the University of Colorado at Denver under the direction of Professor Lori Catalano.

Pursuing place prospecting, Ellin organized a Canalscape symposium (figure 3.7), featuring presentations from experts on water policy, land use, hydrology, real estate development, and canal history. In addition, artists and designers pre-

Figure 3.7 The Canalscape symposium at ASU's Downtown Campus (Credit: Nan Ellin)

sented public art constructed along the canals as well as visions for art and urban design along them. The symposium prompted a major editorial in the *Arizona Republic* describing Canalscape as "a marvelous little plan to make us all face— and once again take some pleasure from—the single most valuable commodity in the desert, our flowing water." This opportunity, the editorial asserted, "is almost shocking, it is so obvious and elegant in its simplicity" (MacEachern 2009).

The two classes from Arizona and Colorado walked the canals together and closely examined four focus areas: a small neighborhood site, a medium com- mercial/residential site, a large commercial/industrial site, and a huge site north of Sky Harbor International Airport, which could become an important gateway into and out of the city (figures 3.8a and 3.8b). David Sprunt, one of the Colorado students, reported that on the six-mile walk he spied "more than 60 shopping carts, tires, baby strollers, a play pen, chairs, mattresses, and hundreds of bottles and cans. Debris and trash litter the back fences of many properties. Graffiti and evidence of drug use mark hidden and not so hidden territories along the canal. Few people were using the trail during a pleasant Saturday afternoon. In all, we saw only about 30 other people on and around the canal paths during our three hour walk." He summed up the task at hand, saying: "The canal has lost a hidden potential as a place that can help build community and connect neighborhoods, a place where people gather, exercise and interact, while at the same time serving its utilitarian purpose of transporting water and power across the city. Uncovering

POLISH

Figure 3.8a A portion of the huge site at
40th Street and Van Buren Avenue
(Credit: Google Earth)

Figure 3.8b The same site on the ground
(Credit: Edgar Cardenas)

PROPOSE

the hybrid potential of this mostly forgotten network was one of the purposes of the collaboration between ASU and UCD" (Sprunt 2009).

Students researched the history of proposals for the canals as well as 121 other canal cities around the world. They also surveyed residents about perceptions and preferences for the canals and produced a half-day community workshop curriculum to be facilitated by municipalities.

Students then introduced a series of planning, policy, and design recommendations for implementation (Canalscape 2009b), including canal-oriented development (COD), sustainability guidelines, public art, urban agriculture, and alternative energy production. They also produced numerous renderings contrasting existing conditions with proposed canalscapes, demonstrating a wide range of possibilities (figures 3.9a and 3.9b, plates 7 and 8).

Figure 3.9a Current conditions at 16th Street Indian School Road (Credit: Jens Kolb)

Figure 3.9b Canalscape proposal for this site by Jens Kolb (Credit: Jens Kolb)

A PhD student in sustainability, Braden Kay, working with artist Laurie Lundquist and architecture student Audrey Maxwell, developed a proposal for floating gardens that would activate the canals with visual and performing arts while providing produce for local restaurants (figure 3.10, plate 9).

To broaden the conversation, the workshop developed a website (http://www .canalscape.org), which includes a portal for community feedback. The Phoenix-Metro Chapter of the American Institute of Architects (AIA) sponsored a Canalscape competition, and the *Arizona Republic* ran a feature story showcasing the work of five submissions (Canalscape 2009a). The Canalscape team assembled all of their own and the AIA's work into an exhibition that opened at the

PROMOTE

Figure 3.10 Floating Gardens by Braden
Kay, Laurie Lundquist, and Audrey Maxwell
(Credit: Kay, Lundquist, and Maxwell)

ASU Art Museum and then moved to Phoenix City Hall, Scottsdale Civic Center, and Gateway Community College. The team also produced a publication about this work that was distributed to hundreds and posted on the website (http://canalscape.org/exhibit-publication/publication/). In the introduction, Ellin makes the case for Canalscape to the local community, saying: "In our very midst, we possess a largely 'uptapped' resource for elevating the Phoenix metropolitan region into the ranks of most livable cities. The canal system that has long been our lifeblood could also be our lifeline towards a more authentic and sustainable desert urbanism. If we are to stop being the poster child for monotonous suburban sprawl and environmental degradation, we should avail ourselves of the opportunity to leverage this remarkable asset without delay" (Ellin 2009).

The "co-creators" on the Canalscape team reached out to populations as varied as urban design professionals, business leaders, politicians, historic preservationists, museum docents, schoolchildren, and global environmentalists. Menconi (2009) describes the breadth of partnerships cultivated for the project as "everyone in town." As Kay (2011) explains, the process "is about taking an idea, refining it, and letting it spread to see what forms it takes," a sort of "campaign to get planners, developers, and city development interested in the idea."

Perhaps the most surprising support came from the Salt River Project (SRP), the local utility chartered to manage the canals by the federal government (which owns the canals). SRP had an image of being as hardened as the concrete canal casings: "For SRP, efficiency and utility defined the organization's approach to its duty to deliver water in the Valley. They were scientists and engineers, not artists or visionaries" (MacEachern 2009). By accommodating the utility's principal concern that nothing be developed in their right-of-way while generating significant excitement about the project in the larger community, the Canalscape team eventually obtained the blessing of SRP, which funded the publication and became a sponsor of the exhibition. One team member, Samuel Feldman, now project analyst for the Department of Community and Economic Development for the City of Phoenix, explains: "The canal water is, ultimately, our drinking water. SRP does not want anything touching the canal, or anyone getting close to it" (Feldman 2011). Of SRP's eventual support, Feldman notes: "They started out very defensively, but ended up being a big partner. No one ever expected that" (Feldman 2011).

Canalscape is currently in the prototype and present phases. Having developed the vision and shared it with others, the Canalscape team was honored when Valley Forward Association, the group of community leaders responsible for Tempe Town Lake, elected to "adopt" and steward the project. Jay Hicks, chairman of the organization, assured that "Valley Forward is committed to transforming the canals from eyesores to amenities" (Hill 2010). As Valley Forward identifies prototype sites to demonstrate Canalscape, municipalities are considering ways to implement COD, and numerous property owners and developers are exploring independently a range of Canalscape opportunities throughout the region.

PROTOTYPE   PRESENT

If these efforts prove fruitful, Phoenix will become a premier canal city. Reflecting on his involvement in the effort, Feldman (2011) said it made him aware that "we have this fabulous asset . . . this very old infrastructure. When considering how people can live sustainably in the desert, I realized we have everything we need because of the canals." Feldman (2009) maintains: "We can celebrate water, and we can bring our canals back to our collective consciousness. If we could see our canals through our bedroom or office windows, or from a table at a local coffee shop, we would remember our connection to our water. We will see that despite our scarcity, we have abundance."

4 | Co-Creation: From Egosystem to Ecosystem

Cities have the capability of providing something for everybody, only because, and only when, they are created by everybody.
　　　　　　　　　　　　　—Jane Jacobs (1961, 238)

Sealed systems have no future—communication, collaboration and partnership are key. Value explodes with membership, in turn drawing in more members. The concept of economies of scale is over-ridden by the "law of increasing returns" . . . according to the so-called "law of plenitude."
　　　　　　　　　　　　　—Charles Landry (2000, 33–34)

ONCE PEOPLE AND PLACE NUGGETS ARE REVEALED, transforming them into jewels is most successful when done collaboratively. Good urbanism *invites* others to contribute, *welcomes* them when they do, and brings them in as true *partners* (figure 4.1). In the words of Jaime Lerner (2010, 191): "A city is a collective dream. To build this dream is vital. [It involves] a process that acknowledges and welcomes the multiple visions that managers, inhabitants, planners, politicians, businesses, and civil society have of their city. . . . The more generous this vision, the more good practices will multiply."

Figure 4.1 Co-creation: Invite, Welcome, Partner

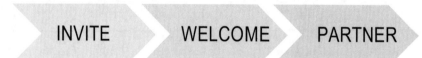

Good urbanism makes a concerted effort to include the rich spectrum of ethnicities, ages, income groups, abilities, and so forth. In contrast to the expert or artist working largely in isolation, good professional urbanists collaborate closely with clients and communities. Such "co-creation," according to Otto Scharmer (2007, 464), enacts "prototypes of the future by linking the intelligences of the head, heart, and hands."

By working together to co-create visions for the future, realization of these visions is already set in motion. As Peter Block (2008, 53) explains: "Once we have declared a possibility, and done so with a sense of belonging and in the presence of others, that possibility has been brought into the room, and thus into the institution, into the community." The co-creative process itself becomes another asset as community collaboration effects a "collective transformation," bringing together the knowledge of many to support something new (Block 2008). In essence, through telling our own stories and listening to stories of others, we create new stories that, in Scharmer's words, "lead from the future as it emerges" (Scharmer 2007).[1]

When groups of people begin **prospecting** collectively, working together to identify gifts, a synergy occurs that allows the gifts to proliferate. Creative ideas and the resources to implement them appear while the interventions themselves tend to have a tentacular or domino effect, catalyzing others in an ongoing dynamic process.[2] Just as good urbanism builds on strengths of people and places, it also recognizes exemplary practices from which to learn and on which to build. It stands proudly on the shoulders of others to see farther through research into best current practices as well as relevant precedents. This "polyphonic" process assembles a multitude of sounds/voices, harmonizing the prosaic with the sacred and rendering good urbanism proactive and generative, rather than reactive.

Although community engagement has long been standard procedure for urban and architectural projects, usually required legally or contractually, it has too often proven futile and frustrating for all involved. In many cases, the community is not provided sufficient information or a framework within which to provide meaningful feedback. In other instances, the proposal is too far advanced to incorporate recommendations in any significant way. This is often described, even by practitioners themselves, as CYB (cover-your-butt) public participation, undertaken for the sake of fulfilling the obligation and perhaps to obtain buy-in. In fewer instances, community engagement is well executed and its outcomes are lauded by participants, but the translation from community feedback to action somehow breaks down along the way. Only in rare instances is community engagement both well done and well applied.

Needless to say, the various professions dedicated to the task of urbanism must also co-create. As architect Phil Allsopp (2009, 1) eloquently explains: "The sadly decaying picture of our urban and suburban situations today is not made better by equipping each separate discipline (e.g., economics, sociology, anthropology, architecture, urban planning, historic preservation etc.) with a better microscope through which to view their part of the problem. Like so many researchers peering down their individual stovepipes over a very large post impressionist image, the telescoping views of the picture end up showing more and more of less and less. The true solutions to sustainable communities actually lie between and among the stovepipe views arguing for more rather than less collaboration, and more rather than less interdisciplinary educational content for our undergraduate and graduate programs."

Speaking to urban designers, Alex Krieger (2009, xii) similarly maintains: "Rather than wallow in despair about the unpredictable nature of decentralized processes, urban designers must learn to be more effective collaborators, willing participants in true interdisciplinary endeavors, and advocates for ideas not always their own, ideas that have the potential to rally others around higher expectations, not expedient solutions. Such skills are not always available in a designers' toolkit."

Co-creative envisioning **polishes** and **proposes** by painting a picture in words and images. At first, this picture is merely suggestive, not too precise, providing a framework that inspires others and allows them to contribute, from their strengths, to crystallize something that is still unformed.[3] Once formalized, the vision may be **prototyped** and **promoted** to raise awareness about the project, obtain additional feedback, and attract support and resources to implement it.[4]

To promote a project, it is important to devise a list of benefits, graphically represent them, and disseminate them. This list should highlight the value the project will bring to the environment (for example, improved water and air quality, mitigation of urban heat island effect, reforestation, reduction in use of fossil fuels, or wildlife protection), the economy (projected return on investment based on comparable examples as well as potential multiplier effects), and the ABC's that together yield quality of life (amenities, beauty, comfort and convenience, dynamism, and equity). A series of existing/proposed scenarios, again rendered suggestively rather than precisely, should accompany this list of benefits, igniting interest among stakeholders and the general public while inciting more ideas to continue calibrating the proposal. This was the advice of Edmund Bacon, who declared: "The real driving force of making a city become vibrant, alive and economically feasible rests in establishing in the collective mind of the people what the city can become" (quoted in Attoe and Logan 1989, 58).

As social entrepreneurs use entrepreneurial principles to achieve social change, good urbanists can be "urban entrepreneurs," applying those principles to achieve positive urban transformation. While the business entrepreneur measures performance in terms of profits, and the social entrepreneur measures success in terms of achieving social goals, the urban entrepreneur measures accomplishment in the co-creation of habitats where people can thrive. To this end, urban entrepreneurs (or, perhaps, "urbapreneurs," to distinguish them from urban business owners[5]) may borrow entrepreneurial tools, such as messaging, marketing, branding, business plans, negotiation skills, management techniques, and consolidating partnerships.

To monitor and convey success, urbapreneurs could calculate "urban capital" to measure the "goodness" of a place. Urban capital might be calculated as the sum total of vitality and vibrancy indices, an aggregate of economic, environmental, cultural vitality, social equity, place attachment, happiness, quality of life, and public health (physical and mental) indicators.[6] An additional metric for calculating urban capital is the presence and strength of self-adjusting feedback mechanisms to adjust places appropriately and efficiently over time. Calculating urban capital could be applied to determine baselines, establish projected outcomes, monitor progress, and assess deliverables.

Through co-creating places, collective envisioning and benchmarking replace goal setting by master builders, revising the conventional organization chart and making process and product inextricable. As Ken Greenberg (2011, 152) ascertains: "A whole new way of working on cities is materializing, and all the old arguments about who leads are becoming moot. . . . Credit for city-scale design must now be spread broadly." It is not about master builders, Greenberg contends, but about people working together, "a strong, deep culture of the city with a widely shared web of relationships, a deep bench of committed city champions and a long collective memory" (347).

In an open letter to the *New York Times*, the Project for Public Spaces (2004) described this evolution: "Ideas, decisions, and even inspiration will come from a wider assortment of sources, including people who live there, work there, or visit there. And a number of disciplines must be drawn upon to create places that meet the various needs of people using them. Architects, landscape designers, traffic engineers, community development advocates, and economic development authorities, among others, will be in the mix, jostling and debating about how to best make a place where people will want to be." Thanks to "millions of newly cyber-connected residents," assert urbanists Carlo Ratti and Anthony Townsend (2011), "truly smart—and real—cities are not like an army regiment marching in lock-step to the commander's order; they are more like a shifting flock of birds or school of fish, in which individuals respond to subtle social and behavioral cues from their neighbors about which way to move forward."

This new way of working on cities figures into a parallel cultural shift that Otto Scharmer (2010, 2) describes as moving from "egosystem to ecosytem." This shift, he maintains, "does not deal with a technological transformation but with a social transformation: the transformation of the relationship between business, government, and civil society from manipulation and confrontation to dialogue and co-creation." According to Scharmer: "The purpose of this relational shift will be to facilitate profound innovation at the scale of the whole ecosystem."

This transformation is apparent in the global business world's popular slogan "Competitive strategy is the route to nowhere" (Nordström and

Ridderstråle 1999) as well as its dictum that companies move beyond competition to creating new opportunities, or "blue oceans" (Kim and Mauborgne 2005). This recalibration in the business world corresponds to an evolution in how value incurs in today's economy, from being associated with scarcity to deriving from plenitude. Describing these "new rules for the economy," Kevin Kelly (1999) points out that the industrial era rendered profit by producing more for less, but in today's networked economy, "increasing returns are created and shared by the entire network. Many agents, users and competitors together create the network's value . . . and the value of the gains resides in the greater web of relationships." Charles Landry (2000, 33–34) explains this shift as follows: "The industrial economy found value in scarcity so when things became plentiful they were devalued. The network economy reverses this logic: value lies in abundance and relationship. The fax, or email, has worth when others have them too. . . . The value of standards and networks increases in direct proportion to reductions in the costs of hardware and software. . . . The 'law of generosity' illustrates how value is created by giving away access. . . . The goal is indispensability which allows other sales to be generated—e.g. ancillary products, upgrades, advertising."

Along with these new economic rules, the current energy, climate, and debt challenges are transforming our landscapes and lives, calling for unprecedented responses. Planning theorist Philip Emmi (2010) suggests these are not crises from which we will recover in a cyclical fashion, but intimations of a climacteric, "a fundamental shift in conditions from which there is limited recovery of the status quo," foretelling "the unfolding of a new reality within which we will be living henceforth." According to Emmi (2011): "We live between two worlds. One enfeebled and corruptly infirm but not yet gone. The other imminent but not yet born. Planning can seek to resuscitate the old or help deliver the new."

This new reality, Richard Florida (2009, 6) contends, is generating (and demanding) a "new geography":

> We need to let demand for the key products and lifestyles of
> the old order fall, and begin building a new economy, based
> on a new geography. What will this geography look like? [It]
> will be a more concentrated geography, one that allows more
> people to mix more freely and interact more efficiently in a

discrete number of dense, innovative mega-regions and creative cities. Serendipitously, it will be a landscape suited to a world in which petroleum is no longer cheap by any measure. But most of all, it will be a landscape that can accommodate and accelerate invention, innovation, and creation—the activities in which the U.S. still holds a big competitive advantage. . . . Throughout U.S. history, adaptability has been perhaps the best and most quintessential of American attributes. Over the course of the 19th century's Long Depression, the country remade itself from an agricultural power into an industrial one. After the Great Depression, it discovered a new way of living, working, and producing, which contributed to an unprecedented period of mass prosperity. At critical moments, Americans have always looked forward, not back, and surprised the world with our resilience. Can we do it again?

Yes, we can, if this new reality, economy, and geography are a product of co-creation. We co-create because great cities are built by communities over time, a palimpsest with each new layer adding depth, interest, and character. We co-create to learn from the past, other best practices, stakeholders, and other disciplines and professions. Like restorative justice, good urbanism works *with* others, rather than *to* (punitive) or *for* (permissive) others, uncovering the valuable nuggets already there and turning them into jewels to enrich our places and communities.

We each see the world through our own cultural lens, a set of ideas and behaviors that are mutually understood yet constantly changing. Part of culture is language: shared understandings regarding written and oral communication. Another part is urbanism: shared understandings regarding the arrangement and use of space. Both aspects of culture—language and urbanism—are dynamic. It is, in fact, these shared understandings that allow the dynamism, providing a strong base from which to depart, as well as sufficient security to make changes. Our professions and other alliances comprise subcultures that add additional lenses through which we see and act upon the world. Co-creation maintains the healthy dynamism of cultures and subcultures, providing fertile ground in which invention, innovation, and creation may take root and blossom.

PROJECT: Civic Center

LOCATION: Various

KEY PLAYER: Candy Chang

MAJOR THEMES: Slow; low; local; adaptive reuse; creative entrepreneurship; entrepreneurial creativity; collaborative teams; co-creation with stakeholders; community engagement; conversations about urbanism

CASE STUDY WRITTEN BY JENNIFER J. JOHNSON WITH NAN ELLIN

Passing by the beige building perpendicular to the Ice Museum in Fairbanks, Alaska, one encounters an opportunity as quirky as the museum itself. A huge banner spanning the top four floors is emblazoned with the message "Looking for Love Again," and chalkboards at the base of the vacant structure host dozens of scrawled comments, pictures, even diagrams in response to the prompts: "My Memories of the Polaris Building . . ." and "My Hopes for the Polaris Building . . ." (figure 4.2, plate 10). The implicit invitation is to contribute ideas about how this landmark, the tallest building in Fairbanks, could be brought back to life.

Figure 4.2 "Looking for Love Again" in Fairbanks, Alaska (Credit: Civic Center)

The public-participation muse is artist, designer, and urban planner Candy Chang, who believes that "communication tools are just as important an infrastructure system as roads, [and] electricity" (2009b), and that "the design of our public spaces can better reflect what's important to us as residents and as human beings" (2011a). Chang's work has been exhibited at the National Design Museum and Russia's Koltsovo International Airport as well as, she says, "many humble sidewalks" (2011b). It is the considered and considerate work of someone "who likes to make cities more comfortable for people" (Chang 2011e). In 2010, Chang cofounded Civic Center, a New Orleans art and design studio focused on creating quality public spaces and communication tools that help people navigate and shape their cities. In collaboration with her team of writers, artists, designers, urban planners, and computer programmers, Chang has plied her trade in Nairobi, New York City, Helsinki, and her hometown of New Orleans.

According to Chang: "Residents are brimming with local knowledge, from the trivial to the empowering, but if we don't have ways to share all this information, then this wealth of knowledge remains untapped and we live in areas that function as little more than giant hotels of passing strangers" (2009a). To provide these ways, she introduced "The Neighbor Doorknob Hanger" (figure 4.3) in *GOOD* magazine's "Neighborhoods" issue (Chang 2011d). A fresh twist on the "Do Not Disturb" placard common in hotels, one side encourages "Please Disturb!"—with

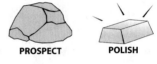

PROSPECT   POLISH

Figure 4.3 "Neighborhood Door Hangers" (Credit: Civic Center)

PROPOSE **PROTOTYPE** **PROMOTE**

PRESENT

best times for in-person visits as well as preferred contact (phone, text, or e-mail). The other side straightforwardly asks "Can I borrow?" and provides space for jotting down desired items. *GOOD* printed the doorknob hangers and included them in the magazine to help people practice the lost art of neighborliness. "We have more and more tools to reach out across the world," says Chang, "but it's still hard to reach out to your entire neighborhood" (Chang 2011d).

Moving beyond bringing neighbors together to affecting change in neighborhoods, Chang launched "I Wish This Was …," vinyl fill-in-the-blank stickers for people to place anywhere (figure 4.4). As Chang (2011c) explains: "It's a fun, low-barrier tool to collect demand in an area, and the responses reflect the hopes, dreams, and colorful imaginations of different neighborhoods across the city." Started in New Orleans, Chang continues to sell the stickers, with sale proceeds supporting subsequent neighborhood public space projects (Chang 2011c).

Observing that people were responding to what others had written on the same stickers, suggesting ways they could work together, Chang's next project aimed to facilitate collaboration. Shifting from analogue to digital tools, *Neighborland* is an interactive website launched in 2011 (https://neighborland.org) that allows participants to work together on conceiving and implementing concepts for their neighborhoods. Developed with interaction designer Dan Parham and engineer Tee Parham, and supported by grants from Tulane University and the Rockefeller Foundation's Urban Innovation Fellowship, Neighborland embodies Chang's commitment to co-creation, empowerment, and accessibility.

Figure 4.4 Box of "I Wish This Was" stickers (Credit: Civic Center)

In a separate project, Chang helped street vendors avoid crippling fines by producing a guide that translates the most commonly violated rules into accessible diagrams: *Vendor Power! A Guide to Street Vending in New York City* (figure 4.5). This easy-to-understand visual manual is distributed for free in English, Bengali, Chinese, Arabic, and Spanish, as well as via the Internet (www.makingpolicypublic .net/index.php?page=vendor-power) (Chang 2009b). A companion piece, *Get to Know Your Street Vendors*, provides information to consumers. To undertake this initiative, Chang was engaged by the Center for Urban Pedagogy, which paired the Street Vendor Project (part of New York City's Urban Justice Center) with designers.

In New Orleans, Chang transformed an abandoned house into a gathering place for contemplation and expression by inscribing the prompt "*Before I Die . . .*" on a blackboard and leaving spaces for passersby to fill (Chang 2011a) (figure 4.6). She was hoping to inspire people to pause and ask themselves what is really important, a question, she notes, "that changed me over the last year after I lost someone I loved very much" (Chang 2011a). Born of Chang's personal prospecting, the project extended to collective and place prospecting through the low-tech media of primer, paint, stencils, and chalk (figure 4.7, plate 11). Gathering wider circles of engagement and support for the project, Chang personally secured permission from the neighborhood association's blight committee, the New Orleans

Figure 4.5 A New York City vendor reading a copy of *Vendor Power!* (Credit: Center for Urban Pedagogy)

Figure 4.6 "Before I Die" in New Orleans (Credit: Civic Center)

Figure 4.7 Candy Chang stenciling (Credit: Civic Center)

Historic District Landmarks Commission, the New Orleans Arts Council, and the New Orleans Planning Commission.

Considered in terms of the abandoned home it adorns, as well as the people who stop by, the work offers a new perspective on place and personal renewal. Kaid Benfield, co-originator of Smart Growth America and LEED for Neighborhood Development (LEED-ND), describes the installation as "merely one of the most creative community projects ever" (Benfield 2011).

Whether facilitating social interaction, helping others imagine better neighborhoods, translating policy into clear language and graphics, or reminding us to live life to its fullest, Candy Chang has been illuminating a range of creative possibilities for the personal and collective prospecting essential to enhancing the public realm.

PROJECT: Envision Utah

LOCATION: Utah

KEY PLAYERS: Robert Grow, John Fregonese, Peter Calthorpe, Jon Huntsman Jr., and the partners, special advisors, and staff of Envision Utah

MAJOR THEMES: Slow; flow; low; local; nature in the city; connected open space systems; network model for cities and regions; transit-oriented development; walkability and bikeability; collaborative teams; co-creation with stakeholders; community engagement; conversations about urbanism

CASE STUDY WRITTEN BY NAN ELLIN WITH JENNIFER J. JOHNSON

The very best tool for cultivating an "emotional capacity to think ahead a few generations," according to Robert Grow (2012), "is to spend time with a child you know and try to envision what his or her life will be like in 25 years; in other words, to get a feeling for the way things might turn out for that child right in front of you." Grow had this opportunity one autumn night in 1995. Driving his son home from soccer practice, the high school junior confided that he and his friends were fearful they would be the first generation of Americans who would not be as well off as their parents. His concerns were about a broad array of factors that would affect their lives. Grow listened intently to his son's concerns about the future of a nation where his ancestors were among the earliest colonists and a state where more recent ancestors were among its founders.

PROSPECT

POLISH

A land use attorney and engineer who was president and chief operating officer of Geneva Steel, Grow had recently been appointed by the Coalition for Utah's Future (formed in 1988) to chair its new Quality Growth Steering Committee. This committee was charged with "researching and recommending methods to address the state's growth challenges" (Coalition for Utah's Future 1999, 2). To develop a process for recommending such methods, the committee interviewed, over the course of six months, "approximately 150 community leaders, including religious leaders, educators, business leaders, environmentalists, developers, local and state government leaders, utility companies, minority and civic leaders" (Coalition 1999, 7). This early rapid collective prospecting was "a critical step in building community support" for the process. It also "laid the groundwork for community participation and effectiveness and generated good feedback about how to proceed" (Coalition 1999, 7).

To implement this process, the Coalition for Utah's Future and the Steering Committee formed Envision Utah in January 1997 as "a nonprofit, nonpartisan public/private partnership that facilitates informed public involvement to explore land use, transportation, and environmental solutions to the challenges presented by growth" (Envision Utah 2012). Grow was asked to lead the organization, and more than one hundred people from diverse sectors were invited to serve as partners or special advisors (only one declined). Led by this diverse and influential group, and staffed by a small group of dedicated experts in community engagement and planning, Envision Utah maintains that its "open, honest and transparent grassroots approach inspires trust, gives residents a voice, and draws on public values, research, scenarios analysis, powerful technology and community visioning" (Envision Utah 2012).

Envision Utah's first order of business was to develop a vision for Utah's Greater Wasatch Area. This region is 120 miles long and about 60 miles wide, with the highly populated Wasatch Front surrounded by a natural growth boundary composed of the Wasatch Mountains, Oquirrh Mountains, Great Salt Lake, and Utah Lake. The Greater Wasatch region is home to more than 80 percent of the state's population: approximately 1.6 million in 1995, 2.4 million in 2011, and projected to grow to 4 million by 2040. To prevent a downward spiral, and indeed to fuel an upward one, Envision Utah embarked on an extensive initiative to develop guidelines for accommodating this growth.

With Fregonese Calthorpe Associates as consultants, Envision Utah undertook a full-scale community-based process, engaging over twenty thousand community members in conversations about what they want for their region into the future. Over the course of 175 public meetings, this process applied values analysis—previously used only for market research—to inform responsive public policy. In addition, participants built scenarios for the future, a tool adopted from the military and multinational corporations, and they also evaluated these scenarios. To support informed engagement, Envision Utah undertook extensive public education through a "massive public awareness campaign" (Coalition for Utah's Future 1999, 24), distributed six hundred thousand questionnaires, launched a website and administered an online survey, conducted workshops for K–12 teachers, produced several thirty-minute documentaries, and convened numerous meetings with key stakeholders and decision makers.

PROMOTE

Envision Utah also studied other metropolitan regions that had experienced rapid growth, particularly Portland and Denver as well as regions in California. As Grow maintains: "The more people we asked questions and listened to, the easier it was to sort out the truth" (Coalition for Utah's Future 1999, 2). The product of all of this work—the Quality Growth Strategy—combined elements from four initial scenarios and marked a stunning shift away from business as usual. Rather than continue the pattern of sprawl, the Quality Growth Strategy opted for focusing most growth in walkable, transit-oriented communities, similar to the compact layout distinguishing early Mormon settlements. As described by Envision Utah, the Quality Growth Strategy protects "Utah's environment, economic strength, and quality of life" (Envision Utah 2011b) by focusing growth near developing cores and corridors, all linked by public transportation.

PROPOSE

Envision Utah successfully lobbied the state legislature to form the Utah Quality Growth Commission that allocates funds for land conservation and planning. According to the Governor's Office of Planning and Budget (GOPB), implementation of this strategy over twenty years would ultimately preserve more than 170 square miles of land within the natural growth boundary, reduce 7.3 percent of vehicle emissions, generate compact development in areas that had been the most sprawling, and save $4.5 billion in transportation, water, sewer, and utility infrastructure costs (GOPB 2000, 5; Envision Utah 2012).

PROMOTE   PROTOTYPE

Since it was produced, the Quality Growth Strategy has played a major role in guiding land use and transportation decisions in the region. In particular, it has influenced development of the region's world-class public transportation system. Prior to the visioning process, light rail had little public support, but after the process, 88 percent favored light rail and other public transportation systems (Envision Utah 2011a). By 2010, the region had constructed more than sixty miles of light rail and commuter rail, and seventy more miles are to be completed within the next three years. In addition, bus rapid transit is expanding and streetcar lines are under construction. The Quality Growth Strategy also laid the groundwork for several subsequent projects along the transit system, including City Creek Center, a $2 billion, 20-plus–acre housing, retail, and office development in the heart of

PRESENT

Salt Lake City that opened in March 2012, and Daybreak, a 4,200-acre compact mixed-use community, where one of every five homes in the Salt Lake Valley is currently sold (www.daybreakutah.com) and the sixth-top-selling development in the United States in 2010 (Best 2010).

In 2005, Envision Utah began work on Wasatch Choice for 2040, Greater Salt Lake City's vision for land use and transportation, with a larger constellation of groups, including Wasatch Front Regional Council, Salt Lake County, University of Utah, Salt Lake City, Utah Transit Authority, American Planning Association (Utah Chapter), Utah Department of Transportation, and Mountainland Association of Governments. In 2010, this team was awarded a HUD Sustainable Communities Regional Planning Grant to maximize transit-oriented development opportunities at six demonstration sites.

Wasatch Choice for 2040 aims to prepare the region for continuing demographic shifts along with economic and environmental challenges. Engaging the larger community in defining this vision, Envision Utah and its partners presented various scenarios with regard to housing options, employment and service locations, and access to public transportation (figures 4.8 and 4.9). Focusing especially on developing a long-range transportation plan, the project explores financially feasible ways to make great places along existing main streets and urban centers as well as in redevelopment areas. This process has produced a series of principles that have become the standard by which new transportation proposals are measured (Envision Utah 2012).

Practicing and refining its approach over the years, Envision Utah has been assisting elected officials, business leaders, and communities across the state and beyond to collectively envision their futures and make informed choices about growth, initiating dozens of projects. According to former Utah governor Jon Huntsman, who replaced Grow as executive director in 1999 (and campaigned on his Envision Utah service to become governor in 2004), this process has "become a national model" (Huntsman 2006), directly inspiring over eighty regions in the United States and thirteen abroad.[7]

In addition to bringing community members together, Envision Utah has also brought municipalities together to articulate and achieve mutual interests, contributing to transform the culture of regional planning. According to leading metropolitan researcher Arthur C. Nelson, Envision Utah has been influential, in part, because "it is willing to take on scary projects that others avoid" (quoted in Envision Utah 2012). Rather than skirt controversial and emotionally charged issues, Envision Utah has entered the fray, successfully helping people find common ground and formulate consensus visions.

Figure 4.8   Existing site in Salt Lake City, Utah (Credit: Envision Utah)

Figure 4.9   One scenario presented for this site (Credit: Envision Utah)

PROJECT: BIMStorm and the Onuma System

LOCATION: Anywhere

KEY PLAYERS: Kimon Onuma

MAJOR THEMES: Flow; connected open space systems; network model for cities and regions; collaborative teams; co-creation with stakeholders; community engagement; conversations about urbanism

"We create poetry with gravity and light."

—*Kimon Onuma (2011)*

CASE STUDY WRITTEN BY JUSTINIAN POPA

PROMOTE

PROTOTYPE

PROPOSE

In January 2011, a swarm of planners, architects, engineers, and geospatial analysts descended on Redlands, California, for the annual GeoDesign Summit. The convention's keynote session was a "BIMStorm," a demonstration of real-time collaborative design on a scale seldom seen in public: in one hour, an audience of two hundred members designed seventy-nine buildings on a Hong Kong site totaling over 36 million square feet and $16 billion of new construction, using only their mobile phones and laptops.

The innovation that made this possible—a web-based software program called the Onuma System—is the brainchild and namesake of architect Kimon Onuma. The system acts as a real-time mediator between a central online model and the innumerable (and often incompatible) software tools used to analyze, design, and manage the urban landscape. An almost complete digitized world in itself, the model can store everything from climate and terrain data to traffic patterns, building information, and input from sensors. This system allows users to contribute to a project according to their inclination and regardless of their expertise, by using whatever software they have at hand. They can even upload scans of hand-drawn images.

Kimon likens it to "booking airline tickets and a hotel on a travel website. You don't have to be familiar with all the complex processes that make it work to use it, and when the flight schedules or the parameters change, the system reflects that in real-time on your computer screen. You can test different scenarios—What if I left at a different time? What if I went by a different route?—and see the results immediately" (Onuma 2011). The Onuma System takes this a step further, Kimon says, because it "allows everyone to access the same information simultaneously from a central location and encourages them to try out alternative solutions together" (2011).

For each BIMStorm, a virtual meeting room is set up, allowing participants to brainstorm and communicate ideas while working on the model. An engineer in Norway might update a building's structural frame to accommodate a Brazilian architect's new design while an environmental graphic designer offers a wayfinding system. Through the system, those changes would be available in real time to the Florida geology student already running an earthquake analysis, and the architect would learn in minutes whether the new design is appropriate in that region. Meanwhile, an artist might be partnering with a social worker met in the virtual forum to explore ways to integrate local culture with opportunities on the project site. The project collaborators could then discuss alternatives as if they were together in the same room. With this tool, Kimon maintains: "We now have the ability to see on a much higher level how buildings and cities are performing and gain new insights about sustainable solutions. Sustainability has many parts and the first is understanding the current state of things, how our buildings and our cities are doing" (Onuma 2011).

Kimon has been conducting BIMStorms worldwide since 2006, promoting a shift toward the open collaboration he maintains is fundamental to advancing planning and architecture. To demonstrate its real-world applications, he has organized BIMStorms on specific topics, from disaster relief after the Haiti earthquake to facilities management for the California community college network.

The Onuma System that powers these BIMStorms dates back to the mid-1990s, with roots in even earlier innovations developed as internal company solutions at Onuma, Inc., then run by Kimon's father, also an architect. Tasked with the master planning of two thousand new homes and other structures for the U.S. Yokosuka Naval Base in Japan, the firm took advantage of emerging technology and the systematic nature of the project to create, as Kimon explains, a set of custom "objects," algorithms that "grew a house or an airplane hangar from a basic set of constraints, like growing a tree, first the trunk, and then you add branches, and then you add leaves, and so on. When the military asked for the deliverables, the drawings and documents, we gave them those, but we also showed them how we'd done it, and they became really excited once they saw that" (Onuma 2011).

The firm garnered steady work on military bases and began building a relationship with the U.S. government that would grow into an indispensable asset. They also started looking for partners with expertise in architecture, planning, and computer systems to complement the company focus on technological collaboration. The "intelligent objects" created for the Yokosuka base helped the firm keep

PROMOTE

PROTOTYPE

PROSPECT

POLISH

pace with the Japanese building boom by allowing its international partners to contribute work on housing projects with no knowledge of local housing requirements. At the same time, because of the constant flights back and forth between the United States and Japan, the firm was also developing tools for long-distance collaboration that would later figure centrally in the Onuma System.

When Japanese investors turned to acquiring properties in the United States, Kimon responded by opening the firm's Onuma and Associates branch in Pasadena, California. This sibling company moved much of its internal technology to the web, where clients could access it directly as needed, and adopted Building Information Modeling (BIM)—software focused on storing almost everything one could possibly record about a building in a three-dimensional computer model.

With these precursors of the modern Onuma System in hand, the company began approaching other architectural, planning, and construction firms, promising to drastically increase their efficiency and cut their hours per project. They would do this, first, by linking these firms to partners and clients with enhanced immediacy, and second, by automating as many of the mundane functions of architectural design as possible. Despite the world of collaborative possibilities and the decrease in routine tasks offered, the proposal occasionally provoked an unexpected amount of resistance. Some companies felt Onuma, Inc. was trying to automate the creative process; others were wary that finishing a project in half the time might mean reaping half the profits. At a few of the larger firms, it was the IT department that objected most stridently, preferring to retain internal control over company information or, perhaps, fearful of becoming redundant.

Onuma, Inc. received the most positive responses from the three groups that had the greatest incentives to adopt efficiency: design/build contractors, owners, and the company's most faithful client, the U.S. government. In 2005, the U.S. Coast Guard (USCG) needed thirty-eight Command Centers designed, a process that took an average of ten months for each facility at the time. "Their existing facilities were constantly out-of-sync with each other because each one had its own methods," Kimon explains. "It's on their financial statements that here's a building of fifty thousand square feet and the building's been gone for two years. And that was not an unusual thing" (Kimon 2011). Using their tools to coordinate between minimally trained Coast Guard planning teams with little knowledge of the software involved, Onuma, Inc. was able to catalogue information about each facility into BIM models. The office also established a process that used the USCG teams to do the initial designing themselves, shrinking ten months of design time to six and earning the company several national awards.

PROPOSE

More importantly, the project forged and tested the prototype of the Onuma System as a foundation for community-based design and self-sustaining projects. When Kimon began organizing BIMStorm demonstrations five years later, some projects, such as Plan Haiti and BIMStorm Tokyo, would continue running on the Onuma servers as ongoing design and planning efforts driven by public contributions.

PRESENT

BIMStorms are a powerful tool for co-creation: "That's basically what they're about," says Kimon (2011), "a non-linear way of bringing people together. BIM-Storms allow us to push it to the limit and try new things. They allow us to fail. . . . The bigger picture is really about collaboration and cooperation." Kimon (2011) reflects: "I saw that opening things up might seem threatening at first, but that also opens up opportunities. We realized the way you advance things for both yourself and society is that you start sharing information, because you can't possibly solve the world's problems by yourself."

5 | Going with the Flow: The New Design with Nature

If we are to prevent megatechnics from further controlling and deforming every aspect of human culture, we shall be able to do so only with the aid of a radically different model derived directly, not from machines, but from living organisms and organic complexes. . . . [The] general name for an economy based on such a model is an economy of plenitude.
—Lewis Mumford (1967–70)

GOOD URBANISM PRESERVES the strengths of places and enhances what may be underperforming with minor adjustments. If it stopped there, it might be Celebrity Chef Urbanism, whipping up dishes from given ingredients. Instead, it may be more like Iron Chef Urbanism, judiciously adding new ingredients that "best express the unique qualities" of a featured theme ingredient (Iron Chef TV Program).

To the assets identified in specific places through effective community engagement, good urbanism adds new ones by going with existing flows, both natural and constructed. These may include contour lines, wildlife corridors, wind corridors, waterways, solar pathways, lines of sight, streets and roads, transit lines, flight paths, pedestrian paths, property lines, and utility lines. Good urbanism inventories such networks as points of departure and sources of inspiration, recalling novelist Italo Calvino's description of landscapes as "spider webs of intricate relationships in search of form" (Calvino 1978, 76). This approach represents a departure from modern planning, which tends to ignore these features or regard them as irritants to be eliminated or disguised.

As participant-observers on the path toward prosperity, good professional urbanists can understand the larger system and determine where there is energy and where it is lacking. They can thus perform "urban acupuncture," inserting new elements into the urban organism that will clear blockages along "urban meridians" and liberate the life force (or *chi*) of a city.[1] These new elements clear physical as well as social blockages along meridians (the natural and constructed existing flows listed above), enhancing the health and well-being of places and communities by bringing urban and economic revitalization. Going with the flow allows places to be "in flow," facilitating movement of people, goods, and information, while also offering interesting, unique, and authentic experience.[2] Urban acupuncture activates underutilized resources while attracting new ones.[3]

For example, this process might opt to enhance existing networks rather than implement Urban Growth Boundaries (UGBs). Depending on community needs and desires, these enhanced hubs, nodes, and connectors could feature a range of quality housing, educational and recreational opportunities, workspaces, retail, and restaurants. Instead of the punitive approach of the UGB, which says "Don't go there," incentives would invite participation in making a great city along targeted areas throughout the urban network. Although UGBs attempt to preserve undeveloped land and encourage urban revitalization, the arbitrarily imposed boundaries can act as a noose, strangling the natural growth and development of a city. In the same way that shoreline erosion is prevented more effectively by undercurrent stabilization in the ocean than by walls, allowing waves to roll in more gently, incentives (rather than boundaries) would ensure that people do not pour out of cities. Positive urban reinforcement, or "redirection," allows for the growth of a dynamic polycentric and networked city rather than an artificially imposed and bounded monocentric city. Not incidentally, "positive reinforcement" and "redirecting behavior" similarly have proven more effective in child development than punishment and barriers.

"Going with the flow" has many other implications for urban design. For instance, whenever possible, good urbanism opts for "soft energy," benefiting from natural energy flows and renewable resources, instead of "hard energy" that is centralized, expensive, and polluting. It also favors "living systems" or "living machines" that assemble the correct cast of species so the waste of one biological community becomes food for another (Todd, Todd, and Todd 1994). Good urbanism also favors LID (low-impact development), using pervious surfaces that provide long-term ecological dividends, including decreased heat island effect. For instance, unpaved streets without curbs and simple infiltration swales are less costly than paved streets with curbs and storm drains, allow surface runoff to filter back into the soil, and absorb rain and snow more easily (Calthorpe, Fulton, and Fishman 2001; Condon 2010). LID also increases the quantity and quality of public space (see the University of Arkansas Community Design Center case study later in this chapter).

Healing wounds inflicted upon the landscape by the modern and postmodern eras, good urbanism integrates functions that were separated: living, working, circulating, creating, and recreating. It also integrates people with nature, center with periphery, local character with global forces, the various professions involved with urban growth and development, and people of different ethnicities, incomes, ages, and abilities with one another. To achieve this integration, good urbanism demonstrates the five qualities of "integral urbanism": hybridity, connectivity, porosity, authenticity, and vulnerability.[4]

Whereas modern urbanism espoused the separation of functions in urban form, integral urbanism reaffirms their symbiotic nature through *hybridity*: combining and linking (or "slashing"; see Ellin 2006) them while preserving the integrity of each. In doing so, it learns from ecology and from past urban forms. From ecology, it adopts concepts of biodiversity, optimization, interdependency and more (see below). From city-building wisdom, integral urbanism learns about juxtaposition, simultaneity, and collective decision making, adapting these to contemporary needs and tastes as well as to the landscape we have wrought over the past century.

In actuality, there are three kinds of density: building, population, and programmatic. Livable and lovable places have the third, requiring some of the first two, though not necessarily excessive amounts. Mistakenly, in the quest for urban vitality and sustainable urbanism, many work toward achieving building and population density, when it is actually programmatic density—the adjacency of uses—that is most important. Intensifying program (also described as cross-programming or programmatic integration) can occur spatially (plan and section) as well as temporally over the course of a day, week, or year. It may be accomplished through deliberate interventions by designers, planners, and developers or more spontaneously and serendipitously through the work of small business owners and residents.

Some contemporary integrations recall pre-industrial ones, such as housing above the store and live/work spaces. Others are pre-industrial with a twist, such as housing above the big-box store, time-share condominiums, the movie theatre/restaurant, the bookstore/coffeehouse, the urban plaza or parking lot by day/outdoor movie theatre by night, and advertising integrated with buildings through murals, billboards, and animated screens. Others still are completely of the moment. Such emergent examples of cross-programming include the office with basketball court and daycare center, the intergenerational community building (combining daycare, teenage community center, continuing education, and seniors center), the public school/community center, the integrated parking structure (parking blended into buildings, retail centers, and parks), the cybercafe (sometimes combined with computer retail as well), the laundromat/club, and the dive-in (watching movies while floating on rafts).

Parallel shifts have been occurring in regulatory, real estate, and business practices. Epitomized perhaps by the Barnes & Noble/Starbucks and Borders/Seattle's Best Coffee pairings, the explosion in business partnering is not confined to books and coffee but extends exponentially and virtually such that online services are developing alliances to garner greater market shares and encourage "stickiness" so people don't click away to other "sites." The buzzword *convergence* describes such technological integration.

Transposing programmatic hybridity onto the urban and regional scales can increase density of activity without necessarily increasing building density, or increasing it only slightly in certain areas to produce a low-density urbanism. The outcome is new hybrid typologies (building types) and morphologies (urban forms) that pool human and natural resources for the benefit of all. Resources conserved include time, effort, talent, money, water, energy (fuel, electricity, and human energy), building materials, paper (less paperwork and less junk mail), space, and more.

Hybridity must be complemented by *connectivity* to create vital and dynamic urban networks comprised of nodes and hubs (the larger nodes) linked by connectors. For places, these translate into *cores* (hubs and nodes) and *corridors* (connectors that can themselves be linear hubs or nodes). We might discern six types of interrelated networks that comprise the larger urban network: natural networks (wildlife corridors, weather patterns, waterways, mountain ranges, and so forth), mobility networks (roads, paths and trails, railroads, airways, elevators, escalators, and stairs), exchange and economic networks, communication and virtual networks, social networks, and networks of history and memory.

Together, hybridity and connectivity activate places by creating thresholds, or ecotones—places of intensity where diversity thrives.[5] Like ecological thresholds—such as an arroyo where water flows through the desert, or an estuary where the sea meets the shore—people are similarly drawn to urban thresholds because they satisfy physiological and emotional needs. Both ecological and urban thresholds are sources of sustenance because they are naturally diverse, dynamic, and self-adjusting.

By increasing programmatic density along urban thresholds, good urbanism weaves connections among people, places, and experiences.[6] Consequently, there is less fear and anxiety, as well as more time and energy for communities to elaborate visions and implement them. By enabling efficiencies and synergies, good urbanism conserves more and wastes less. In other words, convergences in space and time (of people, activities, businesses, and so forth) generate new hybrids that, in turn, allow for more convergences, and the process continues. At the urban and regional scales, these qualities reduce commuting, enhance convenience, preserve the natural environment, and increase quality public space, social interaction, and social capital (trust).

Porosity preserves the integrity of that which is brought together, while allowing mutual access through permeable membranes. Modern urbanism attempted to eliminate the border, boundary, or edge, and postmodernism tended to fortify them. While the modern approach resulted in overexposure, homogeneity, and lack of legibility, the postmodern approach was accompanied by extreme cynicism, a growing sense of fear and anxiety, heightened confusion about optimal living conditions, and a declining sense of community. Demonstrating porosity, good urbanism neither eliminates nor fortifies borders, boundaries, and edges. Rather, it engages and enhances them to reintegrate (or integrate anew) places, people, and activities without obliterating difference—in fact, celebrating it. Good professional urbanists understand that urban systems, like natural systems, must be open to receive energy and thrive, but also need membranes that function to increase movement or flows within them. The challenge is to make connections without losing the integrity of individual parts, providing something greater than their sum. The question inheres in what to allow in and what not, and in what to reveal and what to conceal.

Authenticity and *vulnerability* involve listening deeply to draw inspiration from actual social and physical conditions with an ethic of care, honesty, and respect. We seek authenticity in a place just as we'd rather slip between all-cotton rather than polyester-blend sheets at night. And, as current sheet trends suggest, the higher the thread count the better. Just as higher thread count improves the comfort and quality of our sheets, so too a higher urban thread count—a fine- as opposed to a coarse-grain fabric—improves the comfort and quality of our cities. An "authenti-city" results from a combination of large-scale and small-scale interventions, both systematic and serendipitous. How it happens is just as important as—and goes hand in hand with—what happens. The authenti-city is responsive to community needs and tastes that have to do with local climate, topography, history, and culture. Like all healthy organisms, it is always growing and evolving, thanks to self-adjusting feedback loops that measure and monitor success and failure.

Vulnerability reminds us to relinquish some (but not all!) control, a departure from master planning that aimed to be comprehensive yet, ironically, tended to generate fragmented cities without soul or character. Rather than focus on designing the final product, good urbanism focuses on designing the process[7]—a process that co-creatively envisions better futures and works toward realizing them. This approach recalls novelist John Barth's refrain in *Tidewater Tales*: "The key to the treasure is the treasure itself" (Barth 1986).

Regarding people as part of nature, and understanding that nature thrives on diversity, good urbanism adheres to the tenet that nothing exists in isolation, only in relation. Therefore, rather than distill, separate, and control—the ethos of modern urbanism—good urbanism aims for integration, inclusion, and dynamism. Expressing an analogous shift in science away from separatism, Arthur Erickson (1980, 23) observed: "By ceaselessly bombarding particles of matter to get at the core of things, science has found that, as Einstein inferred, relationship is the only reality." Applying similar logic to society, Malcolm Gladwell observed that social change emerges primarily though relationships, not from power or money (Gladwell 2000). Aiming to build relationships between people and the land, between people and the built environment, and among people, the five qualities of integral urbanism are, not incidentally, also characteristic of good relationships between people, especially connectivity, authenticity, and vulnerability, but also hybridity (openness and expansiveness) and porosity (maintaining self-integrity while forming new bonds).

If people are part of nature, so are human habitats, just as the nests of birds are part of nature. Therefore, good urbanism integrates nature into the built environment. This is sometimes described as "biophilia"[8] or "permaculture design." Integrating nature may involve bringing nature back through "reforestation" or "reclamation," after a place has been "fragmented" or "desertified." (Fragmentation and desertification result from loss of biodiversity and productivity due to climate change or unsustainable human activities, such as overcultivation, overgrazing, deforestation, and poor irrigation practices.)

Assessing the contemporary landscape of sprawl, Peter Rowe (1992) recommends giving priority to landscape, rather than to free-standing buildings, and transforming suburban malls and office complexes into landscaped built forms to produce a "modern pastoralism." Integrating nature into human habitats generally increases biodiversity, reduces air-conditioning and heating loads, and decreases pollutants by removing ozone and sulfur dioxide from the air. It can also provide shade and food supplies as well as recreational opportunities for all ages, thereby improving public health and increasing social interaction. Not incidentally, bringing more nature into urban regions significantly raises property values.[9]

Good urbanism not only integrates nature but also learns from natural processes. In particular, good urbanism learns from nature's secrets to resiliency. Just as rich biodiversity ensures the health and resilience of ecosystems, ensuring that life will not be wiped out in times of stress, good urbanism aims for urban diversity. As loss of biodiversity in ecosystems leads to fragmentation (for example, when a highway disrupts a wildlife corridor), loss of social or programmatic diversity in our cities can lead to urban fragmentation. Good urbanism thus applies the ecological logic that it is preferable to optimize numerous variables than try to maximize one variable (Forman 1995, 515). Rather than invest one large sum in a sports stadium, shopping mall, or lifestyle center, for instance, it is usually better to invest smaller sums in a wide range of urban revitalization initiatives. In the same way that ecosystem resilience relies on the eco-diversity of a place, prosperous places conserve energy (including human) and other resources while decreasing social isolation and social pathology, thereby empowering people to envision alternatives and implement change most effectively and creatively.

Good urbanism also applies the ecologic logic that "life creates conditions conducive to life, and that is the pattern that works" (Benyus 2010, 204). As Janine Benyus (2010, 203) points out: "Life's 30 million species, in all their diversity, share a small but crucial set of common strategies. These ubiquitous, universal patterns read like a code of conduct for living here on earth. You find that all life is locally attuned and adapted, that it is diverse and resilient, that it builds from the bottom up, is nested and modular, leverages interdependence, and relies on information and cooperation. It performs chemistry in water, . . . runs on sunlight, shops locally, optimizes rather than maximizes, creates with mistakes, and processes in cycles, endlessly reconfiguring a safe subset of the elements in the periodic table."[10] In the same way that "evolutionary convergence" makes the repetition of certain solutions inevitable, such as the "camera eye" of humans, octopus, and squid, we have evolutionary convergences that recur in the built environment, such as streetwalls, multifunctional buildings ("mixed use"), multipurpose streets, and front porches.

In contrast to the nineteenth-century Darwinian notion that evolution leads to fittest design (linear causality) and that thermodynamics leads to thermal equilibrium, good urbanism understands that a system will experience transitions between stable states (bifurcations) and will be nonlinear (because of feedback) as long as there is intense flow of energy and mutual interaction among components.[11] Therefore, there is no "fittest design," nor is there equilibrium. Instead, systems are always changing with multiple coexisting forms (static, periodic, and strange attractors) (De Landa 1998). The goal of good urbanism is thus not to achieve a stable perfect state (or utopia) but to generate places of interest and comfort, knowing full well these will always be evolving.

Interweaving ecological, building, and cultural systems has age-old precedents as well as more recent versions. These include Asian geomancy (or *feng shui*) and Vedic architecture, which emphasize the need for cities and buildings to breathe; the Native American understanding of buildings as part of nature; the Renaissance view of the city as having a life force and soul (Kenda 1998); the early twentieth-century Chicago School of Urban Ecology's view of the city as organism; Ebenezer Howard's Garden City; the Regional Planning Association of America's efforts to offer the best of the city and countryside; Lewis Mumford's biotechnics (Mumford 1938, 1967)[12]; the Japanese

Metabolists' interest in dynamic design (Tzonis and Lefaivre 1999); Archigram's notion of "city synthesis"; and the Gaia hypothesis that the earth is a living organism that is interdependent at all levels and scales (advanced by British chemist James Lovelock in 1969).

Many mid-century architects emphasized linking the indoors with the outdoors, including Aldo Van Eyck, Frank Lloyd Wright, and Nikolaus Pevsner. Buckminster Fuller proposed intelligent membranes for buildings to adapt to changes in the environment. Landscape architect Ian McHarg famously advocated "design with nature" (McHarg 1969). More recent versions of designing with nature include landscape ecology (Forman and Godron 1986, Forman 1995), urban ecology (Alberti 2008), biomimicry (Benyus 1997), "cradle to cradle" (McDonough and Braungart 2002, 2003)[13], landscape urbanism (Corner 1999, Waldheim 2006), and ecological urbanism (Mostafavi 2010), all contributing to bring renewed attention to integrating landscape and urbanism.[14]

Whereas technology long served to combat the natural environment while sometimes alienating us from it, today's technologies are contributing to forge stronger connections with others and the places we live. Consequently, good urbanism does not perceive a battle—or need to choose—between the city-as-organism and the city-as-machine (see Ellin 1999). With transportation, communication, and information technologies irrevocably reconfiguring space and time, it may no longer be possible, or relevant, to clearly separate the organism from the machine, as we become increasingly cyborg-like. Some people have machine components, such as pacemakers or artificial limbs; others depend on hearing aids, insulin-monitoring devices, or other devices; and others still were created with technical assistance (bioengineering). At the very least, we are interdependent with the machines in our lives, from our smart phones and computers to cars, mass transit, and others.

Many of our technologies today are actually supporting—while inflecting—efforts to emulate and incorporate nature. With the assistance of computers, we can now represent waves, folds, undulations, twists, warps, and more, providing a hyper-rational means of representing a "higher level order" that has long been integral to the divergent worldviews of Buddhism, Taoism, and the Romantics, as well as cosmologies proposed by Albert Einstein (quantum mechanics), Arthur Koestler (the holonic), Alfred North Whitehead, and others. In addition to the ideal shapes of classical (Euclidean) geometry, computers can now represent "anexact" (self-similar, not self-same) shapes found in nature, also described as fractals (geometry of the irregular) of time and space and "fluid/topological geometries." Interestingly, the idea of self-organizing change in ecosystems through feedback is not new, though it has only recently gained widespread acceptance thanks to software that can graphically render it.

By allowing us to design and represent buildings and cities as dynamic entities rather than static ones, social media and collaborative computer-based technologies are enabling a convergence of humanly constructed and naturally occurring processes and products. They are also facilitating collective "hive design" and creative forms of community engagement with a wide range of participants (see the BIMStorm and Onuma System case study in chapter 4). Along with assisting the design process, technological ubiquity and mobility allow more organic and flexible modes of communication as well as patterns of settlement.[15]

We are only just beginning to realize the full potential of technology to assist with visualizing best possibilities, sharing these visions, co-creating, building self-adjusting feedback mechanisms, rapid prototyping, facilitating interdisciplinarity and horizontal integration, and more. These tools, along with lessons learned from nature, are great companions and important assets along the Path toward Prosperity.

PROJECT: Open Space Seattle 2100

LOCATION: Seattle Metropolitan Region

KEY PLAYERS: Landscape architects Nancy Rottle and Brice Maryman

MAJOR THEMES: Flow; low; local; nature in the city; connected open space systems; network model for cities and regions; adaptive infrastructure reuse; walkability and bike-ability; collaborative teams; co-creation with stakeholders; community engagement; conversations about urbanism.

CASE STUDY WRITTEN BY NAN ELLIN WITH JENNIFER J. JOHNSON

When landscape architect John Charles Olmsted, nephew and adopted son of Frederick Law Olmsted, was commissioned to design a comprehensive plan for Seattle's city parks and boulevards in 1903, he was charged with providing green space for a city that would grow to a population of half a million (figure 5.1). Seattle reached that size by the 1950s, and grew to over 600,000 by the year 2000, with the accompanying pattern of sprawl characteristic of most U.S. cities.

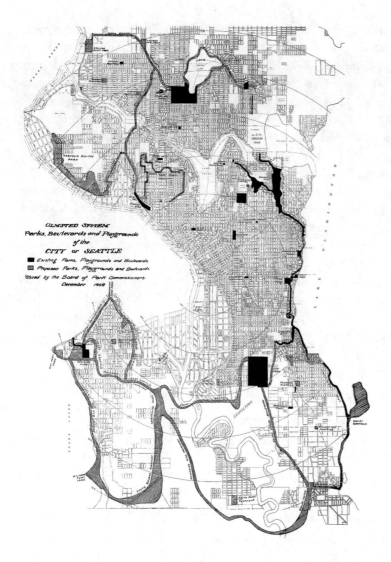

Figure 5.1 John Charles Olmsted Plan for Seattle, 1903 (Credit: Seattle Department of Parks and Recreation and Friends of Seattle's Olmsted Parks)

In an effort to counter sprawl, Seattle mayor Greg Nickels began aggressively encouraging density in the core in 2002. The strategy, however, neglected to integrate open space and nature into the city. While working on various neighborhood planning projects in 2005, landscape architects and professors Nancy Rottle and Brice Maryman were faced with the need for an open space system that would serve a growing and denser population for the next century. According to Rottle (2011b), they "saw the opportunity to address this issue while also engaging our students in powerful service learning."

PROSPECT

Recognizing the Centennial of the Olmsted Plan, Rottle and Maryman proactively initiated Open Space Seattle 2100 to envision the next century with "a comprehensive network of parks, civic spaces, streets, trails, shorelines, and urban forests that will bind neighborhoods to one another, create ecological conduits from the city's ridgelines to its shorelines, and ensure a wealth of green spaces for all citizens to enjoy" (Open Space Seattle 2011b). As Rottle and Maryman described it: "This vision of a regenerative green infrastructure will strive to create a healthy, beautiful Seattle while maximizing our economic, social, and ecological sustainability" (American Society of Landscape Architects 2007).

Having prospected personally, Rottle and Maryman then undertook collective prospecting. To broaden awareness of the open space plan and obtain feedback, they organized a lecture series that was attended by over one thousand people. Inspired by the Mountains to Sound Greenway Trust that was successfully weaving a greenway throughout the larger region, Rottle and Maryman adopted the trust's organizational structure of high-level municipal leaders with "a coalition of as many diverse advocates as we could think of" (Rottle 2011b). They met with numerous stakeholder groups and formed an advisory group comprising more than fifty organizations that worked to establish eight open space principles.

POLISH

Eight Open Space Principles (from http://www.open2100.org/)

1. REGIONAL RESPONSIVENESS

Consider Seattle's role as an ecological, economic, and cultural crossroads; its location in one of the world's great estuaries and between two dramatic mountain ranges; its critical position as a threshold to two major watersheds (Cedar and Green/Duwamish); and its relationship to salt and fresh water bodies throughout the city.

2. INTEGRATED AND MULTI-FUNCTIONAL

Integrate a variety of types of open space within a unifying, coherent structure. Incorporate considerations for streets, creeks, parks, habitat, urban forests, trails, drainage, shorelines, views, commercial and civic spaces, back yards and buildings. Consider layering multiple functions and uses within green spaces to create high-functioning, high value open spaces.

3. EQUITY AND ACCESSIBILITY

Within a network of open spaces provide equitable access for all persons to a variety of outdoor and recreational experiences. Distribute appropriate open space types to every neighborhood, in order to address the needs of diverse population groups. Prioritize public access to water.

4. CONNECTIVITY/COHERENCE

Create a wholly connected system that facilitates non-motorized movement, enhances habitat through connectivity, links diverse neighborhoods, and is easy to navigate and understand. Connect these in-city amenities to surrounding communities, trails and public lands.

5. QUALITY, BEAUTY, IDENTITY and ROOTEDNESS

Use Seattle's many natural strengths to create an exemplary, signature open space system. Build on intrinsic qualities, both natural and cultural; reflect, respond to and interpret geographic, ecological, aesthetic and cultural contexts; address emotional and spiritual needs; and inspire a deep connection to place.

6. ECOLOGICAL FUNCTION AND INTEGRITY

Expand the quantity and quality of natural systems in the city: Provide quality habitat for all appropriate species, with a special emphasis on the waters' edge. Design for hydrological health (water temperature, water quality, water regimes, stormwater), and consider appropriate water and resource conservation strategies. Connect to regional ecosystems in order to achieve integrity, resiliency and biodiversity in ecological systems in the face of climate change.

7. HEALTH AND SAFETY

Continue to make the city a safe and healthful place to live. Reduce the risk of natural hazards (slides, flooding, earthquake, soil and water contamination) while reclaiming and treating previously toxic sites. Provide multiple opportunities for exercise, physical activity, and a connection to nature to be integrated into daily lives.

8. FEASIBILITY, FLEXIBILITY AND STEWARDSHIP

While visionary, the plan should be lasting and feasible, with a complementary set of near-term implementation strategies that includes mechanisms for both public and private investment that are achievable in incremental steps and adaptable over time (e.g. codes, funding sources and incentives). It should be maintainable, inspiring shared stewardship between public agencies, private businesses, and individual citizens to foster pride, purpose and community.

The advisory group also developed a set of goals and objectives for a community Green Futures Charrette and helped obtain gifts and grants to run it in 2006. To inform the charrette, Rottle and Maryman engaged students at University of

Washington in place prospecting, dividing the city into units according to Seattle's watersheds and topography, rather than political or neighborhood units. The students generated an inventory and analysis for each watershed area derived from GIS data, historical and precedent research, and local knowledge. The resulting maps "displayed relevant spatial information . . . , including existing parks and open spaces; water bodies and buried streams; projected urban growth areas; designated transportation, bike and pedestrian routes; land cover and uses; and hazard zones such as earthquake faults and steep slopes" (ASLA 2007). Students also helped assemble a Green Futures Toolkit containing sixteen exemplary case studies along with "an illustrated typology of 23 open space types, and a menu of implementation mechanisms" (ASLA 2007). These resources were posted on the Open Space Seattle website (http://www.open2100.org).

PROPOSE

Over 350 community members participated in the two-day charrette, forming twenty-three multidisciplinary teams of design professionals, students, and other community members, with additional resource specialists available to all teams. Once the participants were divided into watershed groups, preexisting loyalties and prejudices ceded to nature's geographical jurisdiction. This approach effectively eliminated competition between neighborhoods seeking improvement funding for "their" green space, inevitably disadvantaging less organized or influential neighborhoods and failing to achieve the essential interconnections necessary for a successful open space system.

Provided with briefs on each area, future scenarios, and the Green Futures Tool Kit, teams worked to "envision livable, healthy urban watersheds and neighborhoods for the next century" (Open Space Seattle 2011a). Collectively, the teams advanced a proposal called "The Living Lattice: A Network of Neighborsheds," a vision with long-term plans for Seattle's interconnected green infrastructure (ASLA 2007).

PROMOTE

Students then "converted plans from the charrette into GIS databases, using consistent criteria and legends for each watershed so that all 18 watersheds could be merged onto drawings showing the entire city, on both 20-year and 100-year horizons" (ASLA 2007). They also "analyzed the plans to identify a hierarchy of potential connective pedestrian and bicycle corridors" (ASLA 2007). To share this synthesis with the larger community, they produced a 230-page report, *Envisioning Seattle's Green Future: Visions and Strategies from the Green Futures Charrette*, along with an "Implementation Statement," moving the project from visioning and conceptualizing to advocating, adopting, funding, and stewarding (http://depts.washington.edu/open2100/book/book.conclusion.pdf).

The Living Lattice Plan and Eight Open Space Principles were "formally integrated with the city's future planning efforts" (ASLA 2007), and the city has been "developing a process for employing a sustainable infrastructure approach to Capital Improvement Projects (CIP), integrating departmental projects and including social and environmental benefits in their asset management program" (ASLA 2007). The work of Open Space Seattle has informed development of a green infrastructure code that prioritizes green infrastructure expenditures by regulating and rewarding implementation of rainwater harvesting and food cultivation, permeable paving, green roof installation, native and drought-tolerant planting, and tree preservation (http://www.seattle.gov/dpd/permits/greenfactor/Overview/) (Rottle 2011a, ASLA 2007). The process also demonstrated the ability of design professionals to influence policy and inform the public and it catalyzed "a long-term advocacy coalition and planning process to advance the quality of Seattle's integrated open space" (ASLA 2007).

PRESENT

In a ripple effect drawing from collective and place prospecting, Open Space Seattle generated "17 strategies for urban green infrastructure transferable to any city" along four themes: Create an Integrated Green Infrastructure; Promote Ecological Open Space; Balance Density and Community; and Provide Democratic Access and Use (ASLA 2007). Through modeling best practices and generating these transferable strategies, the Seattle experience has inspired and informed green infrastructure projects in Portland, Chicago, Wichita, Washington, D.C., San Francisco, London, and Kobe (Japan).

When Open Space Seattle coalition members were currying support for a $145 million Parks and Green Spaces Levy in 2008, the mayor publicly opposed the proposition (E. C. Barnett 2009). The levy passed with 59 percent approval (www.seattle.gov/parks/levy), and Nickels was defeated in his 2009 bid for reelection in the primary by attorney and environmentalist Mike McGinn, a key contributor to Open Space Seattle (Welch 2010, Rottle 2011b).

By 2012, this six-year funding source had supported the design and construction of over twenty projects, and the design and funding for another twenty, including parks, boulevards, urban farms, street-to-park conversions, green infrastructure, forest and habitat restoration, and playfields and playgrounds (figures 5.2 and 5.3). Details and updates regarding the Parks and Green Spaces Levy development projects can be found at www.seattle.gov/parks/levy/development.htm.

PROTOTYPE

Back in 1903, John Charles Olmsted wrote from Seattle: "I do not know of any place where the natural advantages for parks are better than here. They can be made very attractive, and will be, in time, one of the things that will make Seattle

Figure 5.2 The Hubbard Homestead Park
(Credit: Mithun/Juan Hernandez)

Figure 5.3 The Hubbard Homestead Park
(Credit: Mithun/Juan Hernandez)

known all over the world" (Mulady 2003). Thanks to Open Space Seattle 2100, which built on the strong foundation laid by Olmsted, the city continues to lead the way toward green infrastructure for this century.

PROJECT: The CEDAR Approach

LOCATION: Hooper, Utah

KEY PLAYERS: Sumner Swaner and residents of Hooper

MAJOR THEMES: Slow; flow; low; local; nature in the city; connected open space systems; co-creation with stakeholders; community engagement; conversations about urbanism

CASE STUDY WRITTEN BY JENNIFER J. JOHNSON

"I made them designers" is landscape architect Sumner Swaner's straightforward explanation of how, in just forty-five days, the town of Hooper, in northern Utah, conducted a process that would ensure open space preservation (Swaner 2011). The Hooper open space visioning process engaged citizens throughout the small community, producing a plan to preserve thirty-four miles of bicycle and pedestrian trails as well as seventeen miles of horse trails (Envision Utah 2011c).

Located along the Great Salt Lake, Hooper covers approximately twelve square miles and was incorporated in the year 2000 with a population of four thousand, which almost doubled over the next six years. In 2004, Hooper's leaders decided to address future residents' needs for open space and access to the natural environment, enacting the town's motto, "Preserving Our Past, Protecting Our Present, Preparing Our Future" (Hooper City 2011). To direct the project, they tapped Utah native Sumner Swaner, an environmental planner, landscape architect, and developer with a background in wildlife biology.[16]

PROSPECT

Swaner believes that most open space planning befuddles communities, and he is leery of obtuse procedures requiring a long drawn-out series of charrettes. Instead, he proposed an approach where community members devote two sessions of several hours each to identify open space types in their region and understand how to implement "conservation development." Conservation development prioritizes the "green lungs" of the community, and it involves a four-step design process that is "just the opposite of how civil engineers are taught to design, with open space being the first thing" to consider in the planning process, rather than roads (Swaner 2011).

"For good urbanism to occur," says Swaner (2011), "you can only go to the well so many times." He says: "People need to know that there is a process that will generate a concrete outcome so that their participation is meaningful." Swaner's sessions apply his CEDAR methodology, standing for Cultural, Ecological, Developmental, Agricultural, and Recreational elements of a landscape.[17] This is a method he has been refining throughout his thirty-year career while working with more than one thousand small-town community leaders.

Considering this a process of "coaxing truths" (Swaner 2011), Swaner begins by projecting an aerial map and asking all to identify existing open space in their communities. Participants are also provided with their own hard-copy maps to designate spaces aligning with each element of CEDAR. Based on these designations, they collectively propose a network of open spaces. From there, participants look forward thirty years, considering projected population and residential growth, indicating ideal sites for this growth on their maps. "The sequence is really important, because it helps people think through and understand open space," explains Swaner (2011).

POLISH

PROPOSE   PROTOTYPE

PRESENT

At this point, community participants have completed their first session, and Swaner and his team spend the next several hours synthesizing maps, recording commonalities in a matrix format that provides "content to use in revising open space goals" (Swaner 2011). The team conducts proposed code revisions, aligning with the community's map-generated open space preservation plans. Then, session two asks participants to provide feedback on this synthesis and code revisions, which are then refined and adopted into their regulatory practices. In contrast to the rigor, precision, and newfound "gospel" of geographical information systems (GIS), Swaner (2011) calls CEDAR "a welcome, very fuzzy and qualitative way of doing things." He considers GIS a crutch and—for small communities like Hooper—"a prohibitively expensive methodology for doing the right thing in terms of preserving open space." In contrast, CEDAR is "affordable, accessible, [and] participatory" adding "a tier of simplicity" to open space planning (Swaner 2011).

In 2004, the Utah Quality Growth Commission (which spawned Envision Utah; see earlier in this chapter) honored the Hooper City Parks and Trails Master Plan as a model of "quality growth." Hooper's 83.9% increase in population from 2000 to 2010 and a median income that is 30 percent higher than that of the county in which it resides further underscore the desirability of Hooper as a place to live, and a place where community members became designers of the town's future.

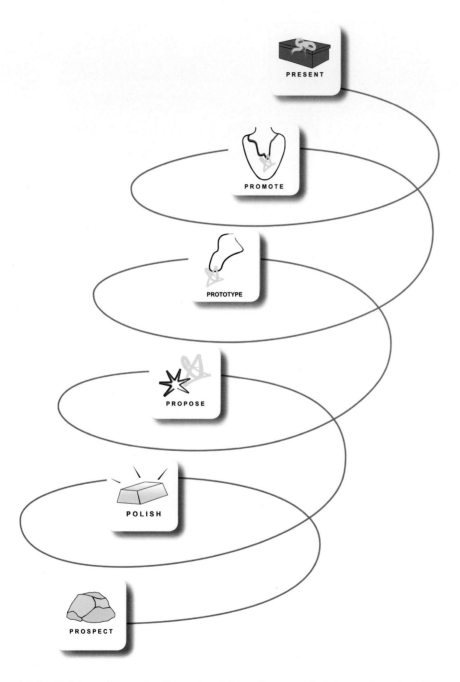

Plate 1: Path toward Prosperity: Prospect → Polish → Propose → Prototype → Promote → Present

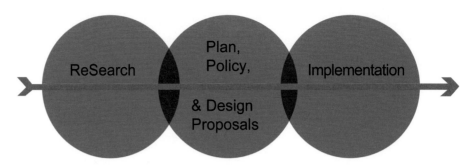

Plate 2: Conventional approach

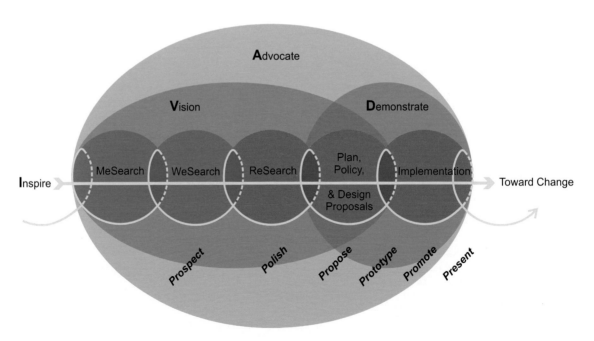

Plate 3: Enriched Approach: VIDA and the Path toward Prosperity

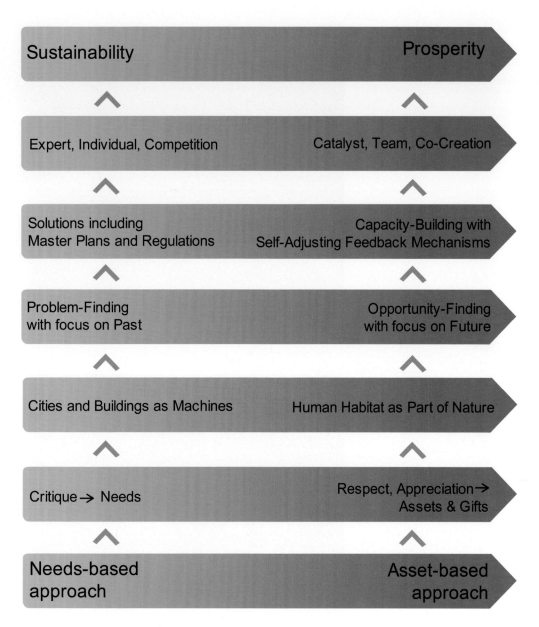

Plate 4: The shift from sustainability to prosperity in urbanism

Plate 5: The High Line designed by James Corner Field Operations, architects Diller Scofidio + Renfro, and planting designer Piet Oudolf (Credit: Master Gardeners of Mercer County)

Plate 6: The High Line designed by James Corner Field Operations, architects Diller Scofidio + Renfro, and planting designer Piet Oudolf (Credit: Master Gardeners of Mercer County)

Plate 7: Current condition at 16th Street Indian School Road (Credit: Jens Kolb)

Plate 8: Proposal for canalscape on this site by Jens Kolb (Credit: Jens Kolb)

Plate 9: Floating Gardens by Braden Kay, Laurie Lundquist, and Audrey Maxwell (Credit: Kay, Lundquist, and Maxwell)

Plate 10: "Looking for Love Again" in Fairbanks, Alaska (Credit: Civic Center)

Plate 11: Candy Chang stenciling (Credit: Civic Center)

Plate 12: Porchscapes (Credit: UACDC)

Plate 13: Shared streets are integral to porchscapes (Credit: UACDC)

Plate 14: Maslow's hierarchy of needs (1943)

Plate 15: Hierarchy of gifts

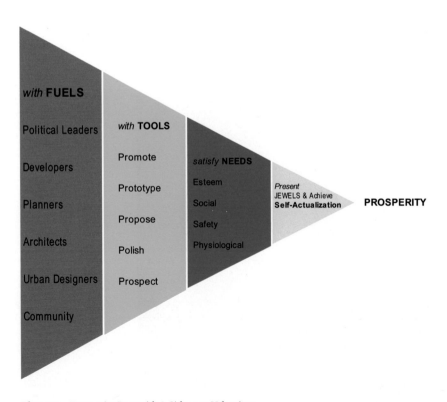

Plate 16: Prosperity Pyramid: A Sideways Urbanism

PROJECT: University of Arkansas Community Design Center

LOCATION: Arkansas

KEY PLAYERS: Stephen Luoni, Jeff Huber, Cory Amos, and Peter Bednar

MAJOR THEMES: Slow; flow; low; local; nature in the city; connected open space systems; adaptive reuse: buildings and infrastructure; transit-oriented development; walkability and bikeability; collaborative teams; co-creation with stakeholders; community engagement

CASE STUDY WRITTEN BY JENNIFER J. JOHNSON WITH NAN ELLIN

The word *recombinant* describes the blending of materials from multiple sources. The University of Arkansas Community Design Center (UACDC) (http://uacdc .uark.edu) develops "recombinant design solutions" by blending urban design, ecological planning, architecture, and landscape architecture. An outreach center for the University of Arkansas' Fay Jones School of Architecture, UACDC offers design insight specific to Arkansas community issues with "currency at the national level" (UACDC 2011b).

More than thirty clients across the state of Arkansas have benefited from the work of the design center, founded in 1995 and currently composed of architects Stephen Luoni (director), Jeff Huber, and Cory Amos, who work in partnership with other entities.[18] UACDC projects range from the conversion of abandoned railroads into transit-oriented development (TOD) sites to proposals for integrating land development with riparian systems ("watershed urbanism"), retrofitting highways to provide quality public space, and rethinking the big box, particularly Wal-Mart, whose headquarters is in Bentonville (near Fayetteville, where the University of Arkansas is located). As Luoni (2011) observes: "Because of our university funding, we're able to take on important issues of the built environment for which there is no voice; we can be the voice that otherwise might not exist."

In partnership with Habitat for Humanity in 2009, the center envisioned a ten-acre, forty-three-unit neighborhood that would "amplify" the potential of low-impact development and thereby reduce nonpoint source pollution, or "people pollution," considered the most serious threat to contamination of groundwater (UACDC 2009, 6). In the proposal, *Porchscapes: Between Neighborhood Watershed and Home,* one-story houses on small lots sited along public greenways are connected by streets designed to store and use stormwater, rather than use pipes, gutters, and catch basins (UACDC 2009, 10) (figure 5.4, plate 12).

To achieve this, the center developed a "Green Neighborhood Transect, leveraging urban and ecological services in the porch, yard, street, and open space" (http://uacdc.uark.edu/project.php?project=40). The streets serve as *woonerfs* (Dutch for "living streets"), becoming parks as well as parking and providing gathering spaces as well as traffic throughways (figure 5.5, plate 13). As explained in the *Porchscapes* vision: "Shared streets deliver numerous social services (e.g., traffic safety, recreation, aesthetics, crime prevention, conviviality) and, unlike conventional streets, do not constitute an environmental liability. The street becomes a net producer of ecological and urban services. Solving for such multiple bottom lines represents the next frontier of housing affordability: regenerative neighborhood infrastructure" (UACDC 2009, 10).

Though Porchscapes was never built, it led UACDC to undertake a related project. Recognizing that Low Impact Development (LID) lacks clear, consistent terminology, the center partnered with colleagues in the university's Biological and Agricultural Engineering Group to produce *Low-Impact Development: A Design Manual for Urban Areas* (University of Arkansas Newswire

PROSPECT   POLISH   PROPOSE

Figure 5.4 Porchscapes (Credit: UACDC)

Figure 5.5 Shared streets are integral to porchscapes (Credit: UACDC)

2011). With funding from the United States Environmental Protection Agency and the Arkansas Natural Resources Commission, the manual provides a lexicon for LID, facilitating collaboration among ecological engineers, architects, landscape architects, and environmental planners. The manual also helps homeowners, government agencies, and municipal organizations understand LID and thereby engage more fully in implementing it. As Luoni says: "The intent was to communicate about a rather unglamorous and complex topic to a lay audience and make a difference in how development is conducted" (University of Arkansas Newswire 2011) (figures 5.6, 5.7, and 5.8).

Almost five thousand copies of the manual have been purchased; the Arkansas Natural Resources Commission obtained one thousand copies of the manual for distribution; and three hundred copies were issued to architecture students at the University of Arkansas. The center partnered with the City of Fayetteville to integrate low-impact design into the city's municipal code, distinguishing it as one of a handful of cities in the United States to permit LID on land that is in the public right-of-way (University of Arkansas Newswire 2011).

PROMOTE

PROTOTYPE

PRESENT

Figure 5.6 The city as stormwater utility (Credit: UACDC)

The city as a natural stormwater utility.

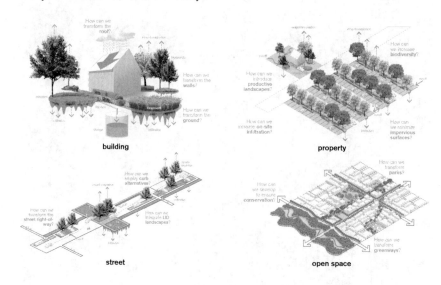

Figure 5.7 Hard versus soft engineering (Credit: UACDC)

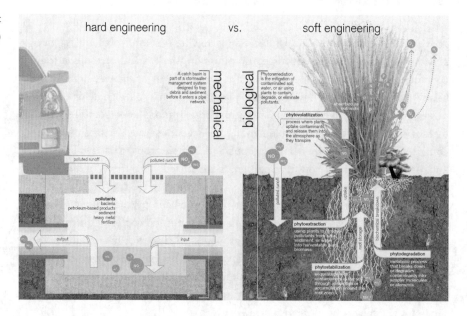

flow control: The regulation of stormwater runoff flow rates.

detention: The temporary storage of stormwater runoff in underground vaults, ponds, or depressed areas to allow for metered discharge that reduce peak flow rates.

retention: The storage of stormwater runoff on site to allow for sedimentation of suspended solids.

filtration: The sequestration of sediment from stormwater runoff through a porous media such as sand, a fibrous root system, or a man-made filter.

infiltration: The vertical movement of stormwater runoff through soil, recharging groundwater.

treatment: Processes that utilize phytoremediation or bacterial colonies to metabolize contaminants in stormwater runoff.

Figure 5.8   Slow, spread and soak (Credit: UACDC)

In an effort to address regional development around Fayetteville, Luoni's instinct was to recall the "underlying urban DNA of a string of towns founded along an abandoned railway corridor from the 1880s" (Luoni 2011). He researched its history and demographic projects—a doubling of the population by the year 2050—and invited students to engage with him in a scenario-planning exercise (figure 5.9).

Based on this work, the center produced *Visioning Rail Transit in Northwest Arkansas: Lifestyles and Ecologies,* a proposal that leverages the early infrastructure to introduce TOD with historic towns as focal points (figures 5.10 and 5.11). In this case, Luoni (2011) says, "the real (public) participation came after publication of the book—the public organized around the issue, because we have pushed the issue out front." Thanks in large part to this work, public transit and attendant smart growth principles have become central to political discussions and debates, including campaigns for congressional races, as well as to planning efforts undertaken by the regional planning authority.

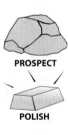

PROSPECT

POLISH

PROPOSE   PROMOTE

PRESENT

Figure 5.9 Existing site and proposed
transit-oriented development
(Credit: UACDC)

Figure 5.10 Envisioning a rail transit hub (Credit: UACDC)

Figure 5.11 Envisioning a transit-oriented district (Credit: UACDC)

Currently, the center is working on two revitalization projects along Main Street in Little Rock. With funding from the National Endowment for the Arts's "Our Town" program, the center is collaborating with Marlon Blackwell Architects to convert four blocks of the historic downtown into a "Cultural Corridor" bringing together the city's scattered cultural organizations and artists into one area. The area will feature LID, intermodal transit, expansion of the streetcar system, infill, and new street geometries. The second Main Street Project, also benefiting from an NEA grant, treats the sixty-block historic Pettaway, a neighborhood on the edge of the central business district composed of single-family houses. The goal is to prepare the neighborhood for repopulation by those wanting to move back to town. The major challenge in both cases is to redevelop a quintessential American urban environment intended for retail into another incarnation, on the assumption that the contraction in retail commerce may last a long while.

What's next? The center would like to develop a scenario planning model to better understand the potential for agricultural urbanism and novel forms of urban design that address food security and local supply. They have proposals into the U.S. Environmental Protection Agency to develop urban watershed plans that manifest LID technologies at an urban scale. And inspired by plans they admire from California, Utah, and Oregon[19], they would like to develop a long-range strategic plan for the region called "Arkansas Tomorrow" (Luoni 2011). Tacking diligently between respecting and pushing boundaries, Luoni (2011) says the center "gets people to think in a radical way—to be more accepting of radical visions."

6 | The Art of Urbanism: A Practice Primer

The object of Art is to give life a shape.
> —William Shakespeare (1590)

The city fosters art and is art; the city creates the theater and is the theater.
> —Lewis Mumford (1937)

Cities have often been likened to symphonies and poems, and the comparison seems to me a perfectly natural one: they are, in fact, objects of the same kind. The city may even be rated higher, since it stands at the point where Nature and artifice meet. . . . It is both natural object and a thing to be cultivated . . . something lived and something dreamed; it is the human invention, par excellence.
> —Claude Lévi-Strauss (1955)

THE CITY IS OUR CANVAS, AND WE ARE ALL URBAN ARTISTS. As anthropologist Claude Lévi-Strauss suggests, cities can be great works of art as people skillfully and lovingly shape them over time. Beyond two- and three-dimensional art, the places we live are 4-D, including the fourth dimension of human experience in space and time. Good urbanism regards our places as potential masterpieces co-created by all and for all to appreciate. The art of urbanism refers to (1) the city as a work of art (a product) and (2) the art of making cities (a process).

The places we live are not only our collective works of art; they are the conditions for our health. Just as we are what we eat, we are where we live because we breathe the air, drink the water, and inhabit the natural and built landscapes. We make our places and they, in turn, make us. While great places nourish body and soul, poor environmental and urban quality challenges us physically as well as emotionally.

Hence, urbanism can be a healing art. As doctors are dedicated to healing people, good urbanists are dedicated to healing places so all can thrive. To be good place healers, urbanists strengthen connections between people and place by following the Path toward Prosperity. A handy guide for following this path is the VIDA approach, as described below.

VIDA: Practicing Good Urbanism

Spanish for "life" and an acronym for Visioning, Inspiring, Demonstrating, and Advocating (Ellin 2010), VIDA counters the tendency to begin with problem finding by applying two kinds of vision: the ability to see things clearly and a vision for a better future (figure 6.1). These are acquired through MeSearch, WeSearch, and ReSearch. MeSearch entails listening to our own intuitions, preconceptions, and biases (**Personal Prospecting**).[1] WeSearch involves listening to others and having meaningful conversations to build relationships, identify assets, and consider how best to leverage them (**Collective Prospecting**). ReSearch investigates the past, best practices elsewhere, and current conditions (**Place Prospecting**).

Combining all three—*MeSearch*, *WeSearch*, and *ReSearch*—enables us to envision best possibilities (**Polish and Propose**) while building support to implement them. Inspiring paints the picture and demonstration prototypes the vision, turning possibilities into realities (**Promote and Prototype**). Finally, the initial catalyst, which may be an individual or a group, bequeaths

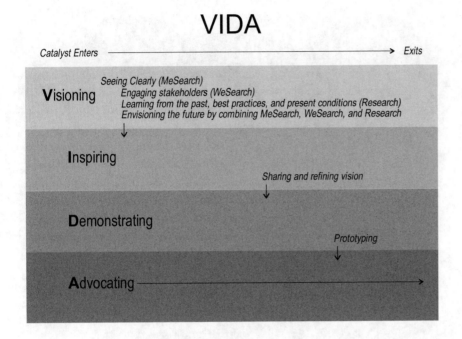

Figure 6.1 The VIDA Process: Visioning, Inspiring, Demonstrating, and Advocating

the project to others who will carry it forward, moving on to catalyze other projects (**Present**).

Advocating takes place throughout the VIDA process by sharing the vision with a range of audiences through appropriate means (**Promote**). Depending on the project, demonstration and advocacy may involve public forums, public scholarship, meeting with public officials and private or nonprofit boards, forging partnerships, and generating long-term environmental, economic, and quality-of-life impact assessments and projections. We must be advocates for our projects. If we cannot share our work with our families, friends, and coworkers in an informed and enthusiastic way, we probably should not be doing it.

The conventional approach proposes plans, policies, or designs informed by initial research with the goal of implementation (figure 6.2, plate 2). Practicing good urbanism enriches this approach with an envisioning process that cultivates good ideas while leveraging the resources and support to realize them. It supplements the conventional approach with MeSearch, WeSearch, envisioning, demonstration, and advocacy[2] (figure 6.3), thereby introducing subtle changes with large impacts.[3]

Figure 6.2 Conventional approach

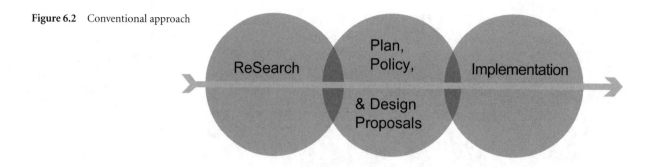

Figure 6.3 Enriched approach for practicing good urbanism

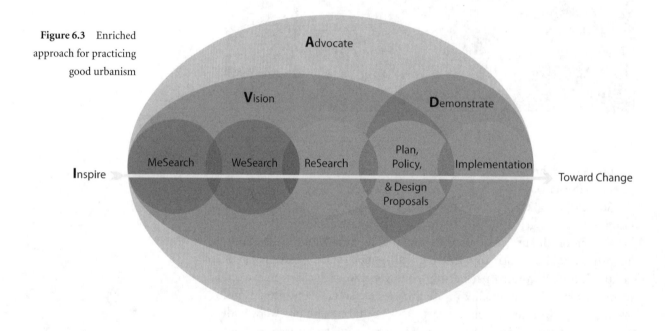

While the Path toward Prosperity describes the direction of this activity in conceptual terms, VIDA translates it into an action agenda, providing a how-to guide. Figure 6.4 and plate 3 illustrate their correspondence.

A critical component to practicing VIDA is conveying ideas to others effectively, especially when inspiring and advocating. How best to construe construction?

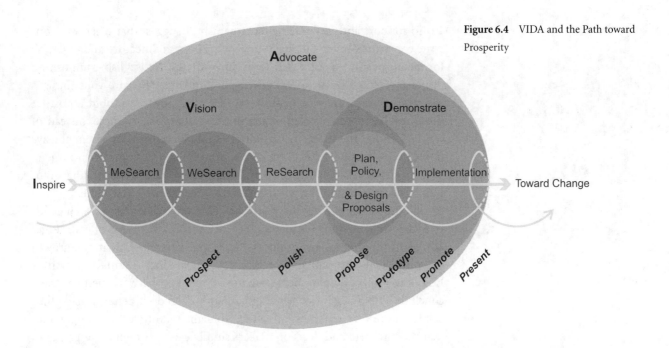

Figure 6.4 VIDA and the Path toward Prosperity

Construing Construction: Aspiring to Inspire

construe: to translate, explain, infer
construction: assembly, manufacture, building, creation

It is common knowledge that positive reinforcement is more effective than negative reinforcement and that carrots (incentives) work better than sticks (punitive measures, threats, or demands). Yet, the literary genre of "criticism" wields its faultfinding saber at literature, art, architecture, dance, film, the city, or whatever its chosen prey. While a critic may praise as well, the primary intent of the genre is—as its name declares—to criticize. Invariably, criticism begets more criticism, for lashing generally begets backlashing, and so forth. It can devolve into a ping pong match with the goal of winning, losing sight of the initial intention.

Regarding urban criticism specifically, the principal goal of improving places often gets lost along the way. We may learn what *not* to do, and also, perhaps, how to gamely smash our opponent. Rarely, however, do we come away with instruction about what *to do*. And rarer still do we learn *how*.

To support and facilitate better urbanism, I suggest that when we "construe construction," by talking and writing about architecture and cities, we formulate positive as opposed to negative theses. As English composition professor George Brosi (1997) advises his students: "Be sure your thesis is always positive. It may be tempting to use a negative thesis, but a positive thesis always represents a dramatic improvement. For example, instead of writing around the thesis that children should be removed from an abusive home, write around your particular alternative to the home environment. Sure it is more difficult to solve a problem than point out that another solution is inadequate, but the positive thesis is much more worthwhile."

In similar fashion to the genre of criticism, academic research tends to focus on something gone wrong ("critical thinking") but offers meager advice on righting it. For instance, studies may examine how urban growth has proceeded unsustainably or how good ideas, such as smart growth or LID (low-impact development), are not adopted properly. Sometimes these conclude with a very brief statement about how to do it better; usually they call for more research to examine the problem; and often they smugly infer that practitioners and decision makers simply can't get their act together to apply best practices. A common occupational hazard of academic research is to work backward from a research question, devoting the bulk of the research to figuring out why something is the way it is, including exhaustive literature searches into everything ever written on the topic. In many instances, the question is largely unanswered, or is cursorily addressed in a concluding section, again calling for additional research. This work betrays a timidity to transfer knowledge into action and to move boldly into the future, taking comfort instead in rehashing the past to explain the present.

Instead, good urbanism begins with a broadly (not narrowly) articulated desired outcome, such as enhancing a place; refines that goal through MeSearch, WeSearch, and ReSearch; discovers obstacles along the path to this outcome (the focus of conventional research); and devotes most attention to offering specific recommendations for enhancing the place. Most likely, these recommendations will alchemize some of the encountered "obstacles" into assets, transmuting them into gold.

The positive thesis in talking and writing about urbanism aims to provide an understanding of the current scene and what led to it, identify strengths and opportunities, share relevant best current practices as well as worthy precedents, galvanize and empower others to contribute from their strengths, convene people to envision better futures, paint this picture to capture the imagination of others, carve out specific proposals around which people can rally, advocate for these proposals and build support to realize them, and then act as a steward and watchdog over these initiatives. In sum, this approach toward talking and writing about urbanism *aspires to inspire* by considering What Was, What Is, and What Could Be. With regard to writing specifically, it exemplifies the following tenets commonly attributed to Joseph Pulitzer: "Put it before them briefly so they will read it, clearly so they will appreciate it, picturesquely so they will remember it and, above all, accurately so they will be guided by its light."

When it comes to communication, architects are notorious for confounding more than clarifying. Describing this "overlooked foundation of architecture: oral and written communication" (Weinstein 2009b), architectural writer Norman Weinstein identifies a source of the issue: "Architecture is in the business of designing spaces for human relationships to unfold. That seems so obvious that you might wonder about the need to insist upon it. Yet just try to find a single architecture school in North America where this truism is the *primary* guiding principle of a professional curriculum. Since so many young architects are professionally educated to be design-driven, not client-centered, communication skills necessary for a successful practice, particularly verbal skills and interpersonal social skills, are seen as *secondary* to design acumen" (Weinstein 2009b).[4]

Some architectural and urban writers, on the other hand, have played an admirable role in raising awareness about the places we live, most notably Ada Louise Huxtable, Paul Goldberger, Herbert Muschamp, John King, and Robert Campbell. Jane Jacobs was also a paragon in this regard. An astute chronicler of urban life, Jacobs squarely addressed issues, eloquently showcased what works, and advanced proposals. In doing so, she demonstrated through her craft—writing combined with advocacy—what she intuitively understood to work in cities: "Dull, inert cities, it's true, do contain the seeds of their own destruction and little else. But vital cities have marvelous innate abilities for understanding, communicating, contriving, and inventing what is required to combat their difficulties. . . . Lively, diverse, intense cities contain the seeds of their own regeneration, with energy enough to carry over for problems and needs outside themselves" (Jacobs 1961, 448). Indeed, Jacobs's insights and activism have provided multiple seeds for urban regeneration by inspiring urban professionals and dwellers alike.

Our Cities, Our Selves

I like to see a man proud of the place in which he lives. I like to see a man live so that his place will be proud of him.
                                                              —Abraham Lincoln

There is a deeper question here that asks, "Why are we sometimes *searching for love*-able places *in the wrong places*?"

Simply put, we cannot achieve connectivity in our places and communities unless we ourselves are connected. As Martin Heidegger (1971) and Karsten Harries (1998) have emphasized, we need to know how to live in order to design for life. It can be hard to create good places, or to take care of existing ones, however, if we haven't been taken care of ourselves. When parents, communities, and places are unable to provide adequate support, it can be difficult to become a good parent, citizen, and steward. And the downward spiral continues.

How do we reverse it and move from bad to *rad* urbanism? In other words, how can we live better so we can design better for life, so we can live better?

The Western separation of people from nature, along with related efforts to control and harness nature for our own ends, is a large taproot of the disconnection. As philosopher Charlene Spretnak (1997, 66) maintains: "Perhaps the most significant feature of the modern worldview is its forceful intensification of three core discontinuities present in Western thought since the era of classical Greek philosophy: that there is a radical break between humans and nature, body and mind, and self and the world." This false separation has engendered many of the problems we now face. The corollary modern urban ideal of the functional city—with its separation of uses, focus on figure rather than field (foregrounded elements rather than background contexts), and clean-slate master planning—only exacerbated the sense of disconnection and separation. The resulting degradation of places has contributed to environmental devastation, social isolation, social and environmental injustice, and a host of physical and emotional health issues.

A plethora of urban prescriptions and self-help books promise to heal what ails us, but rarely do they recognize the obvious, yet oddly overlooked, inextricability of self, city, and site/nature. As both symptom and support of this oversight, our research and practice silos typically separate people (social/behavioral sciences and "helping" professions) from urbanism (planning and design). Yet, there are habitat hazards just as there are occupational hazards. Indeed, the places we inhabit can present hazards to our health.[5]

As psychologist James Hillman points out, a great many complaints registered by individuals seeking therapy derive from actual challenges in their physical environments. It is often, he recounts, those who are most in tune with their surroundings—and its discontents—who turn to psychotherapy for relief. Yet, in many instances, it is not therapy they need, or medication, but better places (Hillman 2008).[6]

As John Friedmann (2000, 467) reminds: "A vibrant civil life is the necessary social context for human flourishing." Human flourishing also relies on comfort, convenience, clean air and water, and access to nature. In *Last Child in the Woods: Saving Our Children from Nature-Deficit Disorder*, Richard Louv (2005) attributes the considerable reduction of time children are spending outdoors in recent years to less access to open space, along with a growing addiction to electronic media and parental fear of natural and human predators. Louv correlates this reduced time outdoors with childhood obesity, attention-deficit disorder, stress, depression, and anxiety. He prescribes "thoughtful exposure of youngsters to nature [as] a powerful form of therapy for attention-deficit disorder and other maladies."[7]

Numerous reports have been issued on the broad range of related environmental and urban factors that significantly impact physical health, such as lack of walkability and public space, and inadequate access to safe places of recreation, health care, nutritious food, efficient transit, employment opportunities, good schools, and a range of housing options that offer affordability, social diversity, and aging in place (Frumkin, Frank, and Jackson 2004, Dannenberg, Frumkin, and Jackson 2011). Recent research suggests, for instance, that the rise in incidence of autism by a staggering 800 percent in the United States since 1993 may be linked to environmental factors, such as pesticides, cleaners, and poor air quality (Wakefield 2007).

These far-reaching urban and environmental hazards to our health amount to what might be described generally as place-deficit disorder (PDD) (Ellin 2012). Affecting people around the globe of all ages, ethnicities, and walks of life, PDD is a prime contributor to physical and mental illness, accidents, crime, social isolation, and weak community bonds.

Hence, it is often places that need therapy and treatment, and it helps to be contributing to administer them. As Hillman (2006, 115) advises: "To improve yourself, you improve your city." The inverse goes without saying: that people's actions can negatively affect places. Clearly, healing ourselves and our places goes hand in hand. Place-deficit disorder, however, can be a catch-22 because the anxiety and stress produced by habitat hazards elicit coping mechanisms that prevent addressing them directly and effectively—in particular, denial, deflection, and distraction. In addition, living in deficient places can hamper the ability to understand the true sources of dissatisfaction and thereby address them.

To restore health to the city and self, then, the deep mutual impacts between people and place must be recognized and tended more fully.[8] As long as we disaggregate them, our landscapes and lives also become fragmented, challenging a sense of wholeness, and severely impairing our ability to link cause and effect, in a vicious downward spiral. We need good ideas more than ever, yet—as urban theorist Leonie Sandercock (2003, 230) suggests—"it may be the knowledge of the good that is most threatened by all our other advances. It is possible that we are becoming more ignorant of the things we must know in order to live well." So, how can we learn to live well?

Knowing how to live well comes in large part from living with people and in places that model civility, respect, and dignity, the original meaning of the word *urbanity*.[9] These places usually weave vital cores and corridors into the natural landscape, instilling a sense of humility, wonder, awe, and serenity. They typically celebrate innovation, creativity, and diversity. And, they have quality public spaces in which we may observe strangers greeting one another, people of all ages and incomes, families, friends, couples walking arm-in-arm or holding hands, some public displays of affection, limited cell phone usage or eating and drinking on the run, and generous sprinklings of music, art, water, smiling, and laughter. Feeling good, people also tend to look good, another sign of quality places.

Those raised in such thriving places are fortunate. But what about those who are not? Like breaking a cycle of poverty, abuse, or neglect, people living in impoverished, abused, and neglected places have to break the cycle, or reverse the spiral. This begins with taking that first step of **prospecting**—identifying personal gifts (talents as well as challenges)—and then the next step, prospecting place gifts with others, and the next. The only precondition for stepping onto the path is a willingness to go somewhere new. Taking that first step, no matter how small, is also taking responsibility for making a positive difference.

Pursuing the Path toward Prosperity initiates a community-building process. Building community, in turn, makes prospecting as well as the next steps along the path much easier. This is because in order to feel more connected—to ourselves, others, and places—we need to feel appreciated for who we are and thus proud of who we are. This sense of self-worth comes from community, which offers the freedom to express ourselves honestly and authentically without fear of retribution or exclusion. Community gives us courage (from

Old French *corage,* meaning "from the heart") to be true to our selves by providing "a structure of belonging" (Block 2008). Rather than "see, hear, and speak no evil"—an admonition to ignore our own perceptions while shielding those in power—the safety that comes with this sense of belonging allows us to see and hear clearly in order to find our voices, express them effectively, and have the courage of our convictions. Instead of feeling shame and ascribing blame, denying, projecting, or idealizing, the comfort of community allows us to trust others, feel compassion, have hope, and express generosity.

The clear vision that comes from being true to ourselves, which is neither near-sighted nor tunnel vision, also enables us to listen well to others and to our places so that collective envisioning can take place. Through collective envisioning, we can produce good places and take care of them.

Everyone has personal insecurities and limitations. Lack of community exacerbates these, while its presence provides a safety net or security blanket that helps all to be calmer, happier, more productive, and wiser. Following the Path toward Prosperity allows all to spiral up, rather than spiral down in resentment, competition, fear, and retribution. Assuming responsibility collectively, we make the shift Peter Block (2008) describes from a "retributive" to a "restorative society."

Rather than cope with poor quality of places through denial, deflection, or distraction, we apply both kinds of vision: the ability to see things clearly and to envision a better future. These entail listening to oneself to grow in awareness; listening to others and places to understand their assets; engaging in conversations that paint a vision of what could be; and energizing all to implement the vision. We can leverage our individual and collective strengths to build on the assets of our places so they will, in turn, support us. Collectively envisioning better futures, we can sustain—rather than strain—life by maintaining healthy bodies, relationships, communities, and places. In the process, we restore connections severed among people, between people and nature, and between body and soul.

When we take care of our places, Hillman says, "we restore soul" (1987, 106).[10] This is prosperity. The price we pay for not doing this, for selling our souls, is too high. To some extent, buried side by side with our urban instinct, is the caring instinct that helps us take care of ourselves, others, and our habitat. To spiral up toward personal and place prosperity, it is essential we exhume them together, taking care of self, city, society, and sites to steward good communities and places.[11]

Sometimes, of course, it seems this journey may take us one step forward and two steps back. That's OK. We can be assured that as long as we're on the path, we're moving toward healing and restoration. As Block (2008, 94) reminds: "We change the world one room at a time. This room, today, becomes an example of the future we want to create." Rather than attack problems with ever greater artillery and armor, we focus on gift finding and co-creating one person, room, household, neighborhood, community, or region at a time, thereby increasing resiliency against problems when they arise and transforming them into our greatest solutions.

Propitiously, this process is already well under way. Particularly over the past two decades, we have been thoroughly reconsidering how to build our habitats. As Charlene Spretnak (1997, 35) remarks: "The emergent perception of the knowing body, the creative cosmos, and the complex sense of place is leading us beyond the boundaries of the modern worldview. Already, it seems inconceivable that we could ever regress back to the ideologies of denial— that is, seeing the body once again as nothing but a biological machine, the biosphere and cosmos as nothing but a predictable, mechanistic clockwork, and place as nothing but background scenery for human projects." Chapter 7 describes this emerging shift toward prosperity.

PROJECT: Sunrise Park

LOCATION: Charlottesville, VA

KEY PLAYERS: Lynne Conboy, Overton McGehee, James Grigg, Jim Tolbert, Bruce Wardell, Dan Rosenswieg, Don Franco, Steve Von Storch, Ryan Jacoby, Karin Rose, Shelley Cole William Morrish, Katie Swenson, and Susanne Schindler

MAJOR THEMES: Local; nature in the city; connected open space systems; adaptive reuse: buildings and infrastructure; walkability and bike-ability; collaborative teams; co-creation with stakeholders; community engagement; conversations about urbanism

CASE STUDY WRITTEN BY NAN ELLIN WITH JENNIFER J. JOHNSON

PROSPECT

When Sunrise Trailer Court, just a mile east of downtown Charlottesville, Virginia, went on the market in 2003, its longtime residents and surrounding neighbors feared they would be displaced by impending gentrification (figure 6.5). The sixteen-unit trailer court on 2.3 acres had been there for twenty-five years and enjoyed

Figure 6.5 Sunrise Trailer Court (Credit: Andres Backer)

an unobstructed view of Thomas Jefferson's historic Monticello residence on Monticello Mountain. Habitat for Humanity of Greater Charlottesville, under the leadership of Overton McGehee and Lynn Conboy, had a close eye on Sunrise after two other trailer parks had been sold, displacing all residents. In Charlottesville—a popular retirement destination where real estate rates have been rising rapidly even during the economic downturn—these displaced trailer park residents could not afford to live anywhere else.

Conspiring with the very market forces that were threatening this community, Habitat was hoping to redevelop the area without displacing any residents, by applying a mixed-income formula whereby new market rate housing on the site would help fund affordable housing (http://www.urban-habitats. org/). Moving swiftly to stall and potentially halt the sale, Habitat approached the City of Charlottesville with a proposal to redevelop the area. After a developer got a contract on the property with a plan to build ninety luxury condos, the neighborhood association protested and the developer backed out. Financial support from numerous donors allowed Habitat to acquire the property, and immediate, broad-based neighborhood support ensued—a likely result of Habitat's local track record of building fifty low-income houses in

POLISH

Charlottesville and engaging in international humanitarian efforts (Morrish, Schindler, and Swenson 2009, 29).

Adding support to this project, Katie Swenson of the Charlottesville Community Design Center approached Habitat and suggested running a design competition. "The project struck a chord on so many levels," recalls Swenson (2011), who currently directs the Rose Fellowship, which works at the national level to advance collaboration between designers and affordable housing developers. Joining Swenson in this endeavor was William Morrish, then professor of architecture, landscape architecture, and urban and environmental planning at the University of Virginia (and currently dean at Parsons), who was fascinated by trailer parks and frustrated by architectural proposals that fail to address actual places in a meaningful way (Morrish 2011).

Habitat and the Charlottesville Community Design Center engaged the local community extensively—the thirty-two residents of Sunrise as well as those from neighboring communities—to bring other voices to the table and to develop "realistic, innovative, universal models for multifamily housing that prevent gentrification and displacement" (http://www.urban-habitats.org). According to the competition brief for "Urban Habitats: Seeking a New Housing Development Model," proposals should "generate culturally and climatically responsive architecture through a sustainable continuum, from site development to energy efficient unit operation" (http://www.urban-habitats.org). One hundred and sixty-four entries arrived from fifty-two countries, and the competition was juried by the late J. Max Bond, along with Teddy Cruz, Julie Eizenberg, and representatives from Habitat for Humanity, the local American Institute of Architects, and the city council. The jury spent time with residents from the area who showed them around and shared their criteria for redevelopment: preservation of the big "back yard" for communal use, including a community garden; architecture and site design that fit into the fabric of the greater neighborhood; and use of green building techniques.

PROPOSE

The jury selected three winners and the community awarded an additional "People's Choice." The juror who ultimately influenced selection of the overall winning entry was Sunrise resident Marion Dudley. "Through this process [she] emerged as a voice of the community," recalls Swenson (2011). When the judges had narrowed the entries down to the last three, Dudley, who had initially required guidance through each submission by the professionals on hand, "finally put a stake in the ground, pointing to the one that really spoke to her. It was a teaching moment for all of us," notes Swenson (2011). Dudley's choice, "Double Wide, Triple High" by the firm Genter Schindler, raised ceilings to ten feet or higher, maximizing the benefits of cross-ventilation and natural light and providing unique indoor and outdoor spaces to each unit (figure 6.6). More significantly, the site plan respected the existing central street, which served as the community spine and gathering place.

Most projects exemplified the tenet of second-place winner Metropolitan Planning Collaborative (NYC): "Re-new, don't re-invent" (http://www.urban-habitats .org). As Aaron Young, one of the five members of this team, describes their entry: "The Sunrise plan seeks to leverage the trailer park's assets—a strong sense of community, compact housing, multiple and flexible use of open space, and a spectacular mountain view. Additionally, the Sunrise plan aims to leverage existing infrastructure—sanitary layout, internal vehicular circulation patterns, and trees—

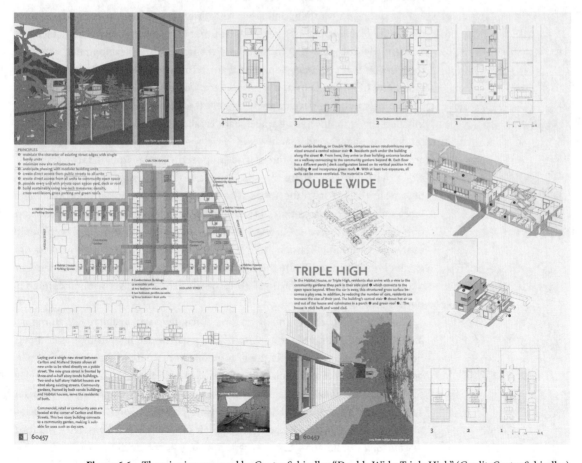

Figure 6.6   The winning proposal by Genter Schindler, "Double Wide, Triple High" (Credit: Genter Schindler)

PROMOTE

while better weaving the block into the physical fabric of the larger neighborhood" (http://www.urban-habitats.org).

The Charlottesville Community Design Center hosted an *Urban Habitats* exhibition along with a conference that explored prospects for compact and affordable housing (Morrish, Schindler, and Swenson 2009, 17). A member of the first-place team, Susanne Schindler, became so involved in the project that she joined Swenson and Morrish to co-author *Growing Urban Habitats*, a "source book and a how-to guide" for retrofitting lower-density urban areas with mixed-income higher-density development (Morrish et al. 2009, 22, 24). The book presents the Sunrise proposals along with such others as Fung + Blatt's CityHoodHomes for Los Angeles, Portland's Living Smart Project by Vargas Greenan Architects, and high-density infill in North Philadelphia's Onion Flats' Rag Flats.

According to Morrish, Schindler, and Swenson (2009, 69): "The success of the *Urban Habitats* process lies in its affirmation of community-based collaboration and design. Last year, neighbors were fighting the development; this year, they are part of the redevelopment team." To design Sunrise Park, Habitat for Humanity hired the first- and second-place winners of the competition to assist with "a new housing development model" (Morrish et al. 2009, 17) and in 2009 initiated the rezoning of the trailer park to allow mixed-use development. Habitat then engaged land planner and developer Community Results along with architects Stoneking Von Storch, who proposed "single-family attached houses" along the south side where the site fronts a residential street with small houses built from the 1920s to the 1950s. The buildings in the northern portion, which faces a commercial street, are larger and more contemporary. Community support and interest were so strong that Habitat was able to include a community center, a community garden, "pervious roads and sidewalks, a networked rain catchment system to irrigate the common area with rainwater, enhanced rain gardens and energy efficient fixtures" (http://cvillehabitat.org/sunrise), all funded by donors.

PROTOTYPE

Thanks to the commitment and resourcefulness of Habitat for Humanity, along with the additional momentum and creativity generated by the competition and exhibition, Sunrise is the first mobile home park in the United States to be redeveloped without displacing any residents. Of the original sixteen families, nine elected to remain in the neighborhood and will be renting newly constructed apartments for no more than what they were paying previously (in some cases, nothing) and never above 30 percent of their gross family income. They will form the nucleus of the larger Sunrise Park, which will include sixty-six units of townhouses, condos, and apartments when it is completed in 2014. Half of the units will be affordable, and half will be market rate.

McGehee, who moved on in 2008 to head up Habitat for Humanity Virginia, said: "I think we're so fortunate because the folks who live there are a tightly knit community and will form the core of a larger tightly-knit community. . . . They all check on each other every day. That is the wonderful neighborhood we're building around" (McGehee 2005). Dan Rosensweig, currently at the helm of Charlottesville Habitat, remarks: "The residents of the park—our most cherished partners—seem to be very happy with the process and are looking forward to moving into their new homes within a couple of months" (Rosensweig 2012).

Building on the Sunrise experience, Habitat of Greater Charlottesville acquired the significantly larger mobile home park of Southwood, comprising 348 mobile homes on one hundred acres, once again to protect the residents while also taking advantage of development opportunities. Habitat International regards the Sunrise and Southwood initiatives as models for others across the country to emulate.

PRESENT

PROJECT: Groundwork

LOCATION: Ballpark District of Minneapolis, MN

KEY PLAYERS: Mary deLaittre, Peter McLaughlin, Chuck Leer, and Mark Oyaas

MAJOR THEMES: Flow; local; nature in the city; connected open space systems; adaptive reuse; transit-oriented development; walkability and bike-ability; entrepreneurial creativity; collaborative teams; co-creation with stakeholders; community engagement; conversations about urbanism

CASE STUDY WRITTEN BY JENNIFER J. JOHNSON WITH NAN ELLIN

Target Field, home to the Minnesota Twins, is located on the edge of downtown Minneapolis on a former brownfield site, which has been remediated to include a massive cistern and bioswales that convert stormwater into irrigation. Designed by architectural firm HOK, the ballpark was lauded as "an architectural triumph, perhaps the best of the new generation of cozy urban baseball venues" (Berg 2008). It was awarded LEED® Silver Certification and is considered "the Greenest ballpark in America" (MLB.com 2010).

In addition to these green building attributes, Target Field integrates with the surrounding area more successfully than the Twins' former home (the Metrodome), Central Library, and other public buildings in Minneapolis. As Steve Berg, urban affairs columnist for the *Minneapolis Post*, asserted, the city is "infamous for failing, in any pleasing way, to fit these architectural gems into their urban surroundings" (Berg 2008). Bucking this trend, Target Field is "the hub for a variety of public transportation options, including rail, bike and bus routes" (MLB .com 2010), and it was voted by fans as the number-one ballpark in America in its first year (ESPN the Magazine 2010). How did this occur?

PROSPECT

Given the previous urban blunders, local architect Mary deLaittre was concerned the stadium "had the potential of being a UFO just landing in the Minneapolis downtown" (deLaittre 2011). She contacted Hennepin county commissioner Peter McLaughlin, urging him not to allow this new project to become another missed opportunity. McLaughlin, a contributor to Minneapolis's Sustainable Communities Grant from the U.S. Department of Housing and Urban Development, replied by expressing an interest in having "a voice for design at the table" (McLaughlin 2011). DeLaittre and her firm Groundwork: The Foundation for City Building ultimately became this voice. They envisioned transforming an industrial area to a new urban center, building on existing assets to create a well-connected place where the whole would be greater than the sum of its parts.

POLISH

Key to this transformation was engaging stakeholders and getting them to collaborate, educating the public, cultivating support for the approach, and bringing design to the process from the start. To achieve these goals, deLaittre worked with local developer Chuck Leer, public affairs consultant Mark Oyaas, and Peter McLaughlin to cofound the stakeholder group 2010 Partners (now 2020 Partners), an organization cultivating community support and advocating for good city building (http://the2020partners.com). Chaired by Leer, and run by a steering committee, this group included representatives from the city, county, ballpark authority, Minnesota Department of Transportation (MnDOT), neighborhood and civic groups, and Hines Interests, the dominant real estate firm. The Partners grew over 150-strong within the first two years.

Once established, 2010 Partners sponsored an intensive two-day charrette in April 2009 led by urban designer William R. Morrish (2010 Partners, 2009) (see Sunrise Park case study). Morrish, who had previously taught at the University of Minnesota and "still spoke Minneapolan" (Morrish 2011), had the volunteer participants "repeatedly walking the district to understand the myriad projects planned and underway on multiple levels of the city—ground, street and skyway levels" (2010 Partners, 2009). This workshop produced one- and five-year work plans along with a four-step implementation process and timeline, all clearly presented in the pamphlet "Opening Day and Beyond: Leveraging Our Assets to Create Community Connections" (2010 Partners, 2009), which concludes with the message "Run with it!".

What quickly developed from this exercise was the concept of leveraging a "green convergence" of baseball, energy generation, and a smart transportation interchange transforming the preexisting jumble into a sensible framework. "What makes this convergence interesting," explains deLaittre (2011), "is that these assets already existed, and we were just building on them. HERC was there, the transportation lines were there, and the ballpark was there, but nothing was done to make them something greater than the sum of their parts." McLaughlin (2011) recalls that, while participating in this process, he began to realize that "this notion of a district around the ballpark—It wasn't *just* the ballpark. It wasn't even *just about baseball*."

Essential to this convergence was reimagining the Hennepin Energy Recovery Center (HERC), a waste-to-energy facility, as a district-wide energy source providing electricity to the city and heating and cooling to local businesses, as well as a large-scale potential landmark building and source of identity for the district (deLaittre 2011). HERC uses one third of the garbage of Hennepin County to power twenty-five thousand Minneapolis homes through waste-to-energy processes (Schumacher 2011). It prevents hauling garbage to methane-producing landfills and reduces the amount of coal power brought into the city.

This convergence also relied on the transportation interchange, multiple modes of transportation over three levels and five city blocks. "The dialogue about this issue was important," said McLaughlin (2011), and "the bigger-picture idea caught on," helping attract a $4 million gift from the Target Corporation as well as powerful advocates such as Congressman Jim Oberstar, who had served seventeen terms on the House Transportation Committee and fifteen years as the senior Democrat on the House Committee on Transportation and Infrastructure (Goldmark 2010).

Promoting these concepts required collateral materials. One of these was a presentation about the transportation interchange concept that "went everywhere" (deLaittre 2011): to politicians, corporations, neighbors, and others. As deLaittre

PROMOTE

(2011) recalls: "No one knew what a transportation interchange was, let alone how to create one." McLaughlin (2011) points out: "This [work] was before TOD was commonplace in the Midwest" and before "green building" became a household term. Early in the process, deLaittre worked with Oyaas and Leer to create City Building, an educational component to clearly convey the process, basic design principles, initial urban design concepts, and steps to implementation (http://groundworkcitybuilding.com/docs/DAG.pdf). Another tool for communicating the vision was the pamphlet about HERC, "Creating an Energy District," aimed at transforming the public perception of the facility from a "pollution-spewing garbage burner" to a forward-thinking community amenity.[12] This pamphlet also explained how to adjust city plans accordingly, build the necessary infrastructure, and communicate along the way with all involved.

PROTOTYPE

PRESENT

Thanks to 2010/2020 Partners, the concepts garnered interest and support from ever-widening circles. March 27, 2010, was the opening day of Target Field and, although the ambitious "green triad" of entertainment, transportation, and energy has not yet been fully realized, the process of engaging the larger district and its stakeholders managed to "go beyond the footprint of the ballpark and the footprint of baseball and energize that portion of the city as an extension of downtown" (McLaughlin 2011). As a result of these efforts, Target Field has become "the most multi-modal, transit-oriented ballpark in America" (MLB.com 2010) (figure 6.7). HERC is planning to provide heating and cooling to the neighborhood and has applied for a conditional use permit to accept more garbage. The transportation interchange has secured partial funding ($30 million) and responded to a request for proposals for additional funding. And 2020 Partners continues to be an invaluable organization, bringing people together to co-create their city and advocating for locating the Minnesota Vikings Stadium in the neighborhood.

Figure 6.7 The convergence of Target Field, HERC, and transportation interchange (Credit: Mary deLaittre)

7 | From Good to Great Urbanism: Beyond Sustainability to Prosperity

The polis originates . . . in the bare needs of life, and continues in existence for the sake of a good life.

—Aristotle, Politics

We have adopted as a species a strategy of tragedy and if we don't adopt a strategy of hope for our children, they're going to wonder what we were doing.

—William McDonough (2011)

A SIGNIFICANT SHIFT HAS BEEN UNDER WAY GLOBALLY, emerging from broad-based sustainability efforts that have enhanced the quality of our places in recent decades. Thanks to these strides, we are now taking the next step, with an even smaller ecological footprint, moving beyond sustainability to prosperity. While sustainability is certainly an improvement over decline, better still are flourishing, thriving, and prospering. How are we moving in this direction, and how might we accelerate that movement?

As described earlier, the point of departure for the Path toward Prosperity is recognizing assets, in contrast to the prevailing tendency of the past century to begin with problems or deficits. The latter tendency is demonstrated, for instance, by Abraham Maslow's hierarchy of needs (figure 7.1, plate 14). Introduced in 1943, Maslow's pyramid implies that people have deficits that need to be filled, typically by experts, instead of having intrinsic qualities and abilities that can be developed.[1]

Figure 7.1 Maslow's hierarchy of needs (1943)

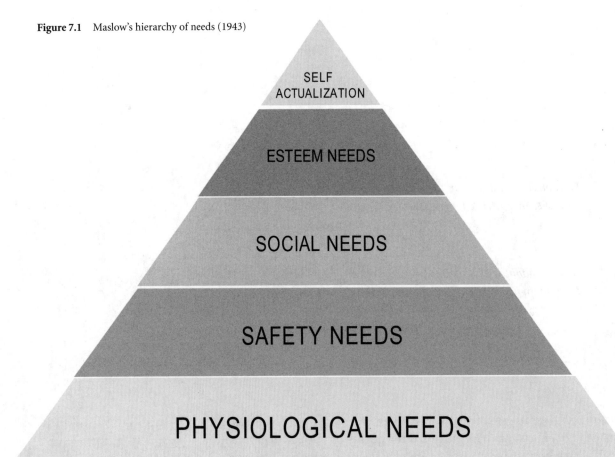

Alternatively, a hierarchy of gifts (figure 7.2, plate 15) describes the prosperity paradigm. From Fuels at the base (sun, water, food, wind, fossil fuels, and other energy sources) and Tools above (knowledge, intuition, and skills; construction, machine, and digital tools; and communication, transportation, and building technologies), the hierarchy of gifts suggests, we can extract Jewels.

The sustainability paradigm aligns with the needs-based approach since it begins by identifying a need or problem and then proposes a solution, establishes goals, and attempts to implement them. Indeed, the most widely applied definition of sustainability includes the word *needs* twice: "Meet-

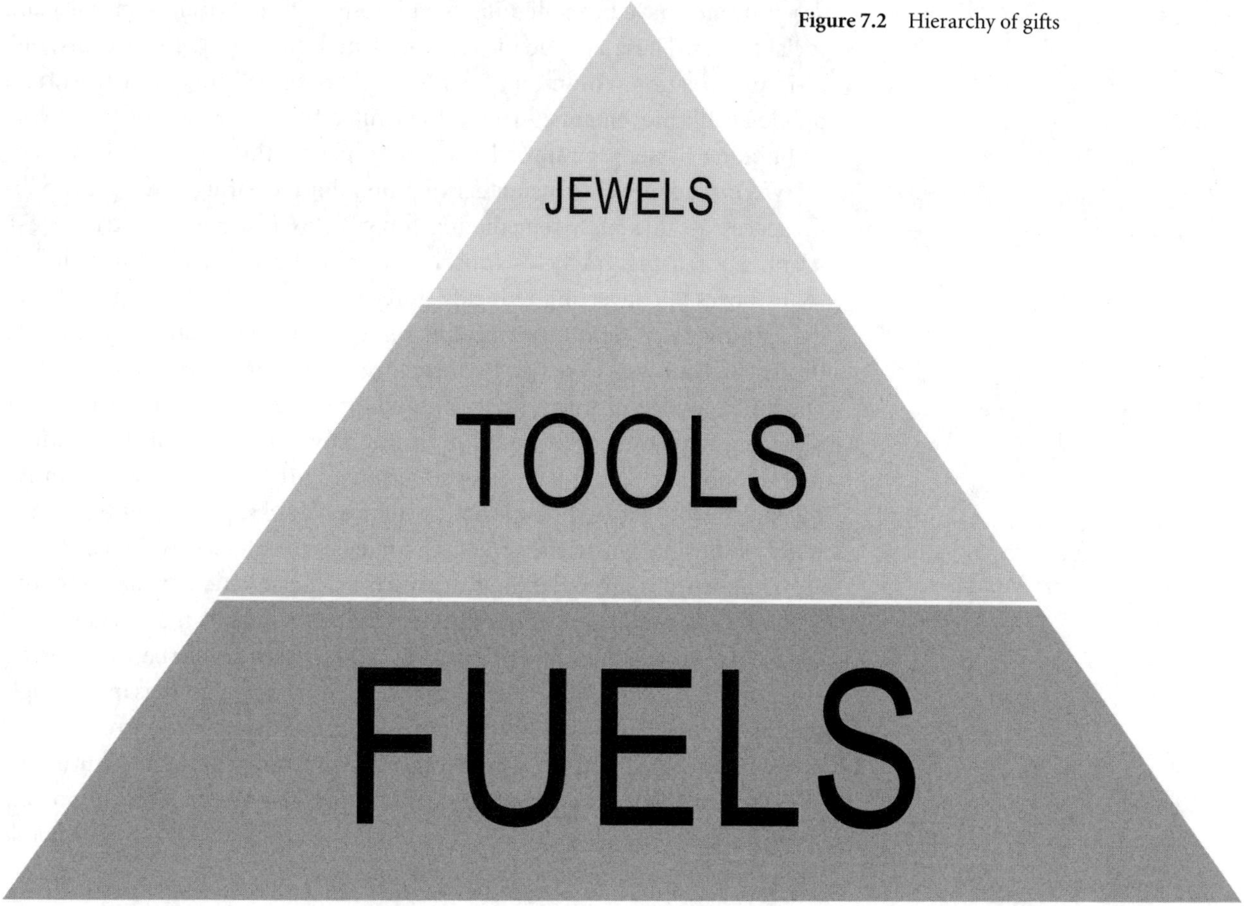

Figure 7.2 Hierarchy of gifts

ing the *needs* of the present without compromising the ability of future generations to meet their own *needs*" (United Nations 1987, emphasis added). In contrast, the prosperity paradigm begins by recognizing assets and then connects them and adds energy to the system through catalytic interventions that recognize the whole, including a self-adjusting feedback mechanism to monitor and effect change (figure 7.3, plate 4). By shifting attention from problem solving to opportunity finding,[2] and by addressing problems from a larger context that engages more people with an attitude of respect and appreciation, this approach becomes yet another gift, a tool for extracting jewels.

This is an exciting historical moment. Despite remaining potholes and blind corners along the path, the shift to prosperity is apparent as urban design trends have been aligning fortuitously with political, economic, and social trends. These include the environmental, smart city, creative city, historic preservation, community garden, urban agriculture, land trust, and public health movements. Around the United States, we have been reviving or building passenger railroad systems, implementing extensive new transit systems, adaptively reusing existing buildings, creating some great public spaces at all scales, remediating brownfields (former industrial sites), adaptively reusing grayfields (obsolescent buildings, often "dead malls" or "ghostboxes"), converting redfields (foreclosed properties) into greenfields, daylighting rivers and streams, and undertaking significant initiatives to protect air and water quality. Performance- and form-based guidelines that encourage walkability and integrating nature into the city are increasingly replacing regulations that focus on traffic flow and risk mitigation. Much new development and many older suburbs and urban cores have been introducing transit-oriented development, park networks, permaculture, neighborhood business districts, and other strategies to enhance livability.

These strides are redefining urbanity. Programmatic density (horizontal and vertical mixed use) has been emerging in suburban areas and small towns (Dunham-Jones and Williamson 2008), and new urban infill is far superior to that of prior decades. At the same time, agriculture is increasingly appearing in urban and suburban areas, reducing the need to purchase food at groceries while increasing availability and consumption of local produce. Whether city, suburb, or countryside, farming may coexist with importing food, local businesses with global ones, and mass transit with the automobile or perhaps even automated Personal Rapid Transit (PRT).

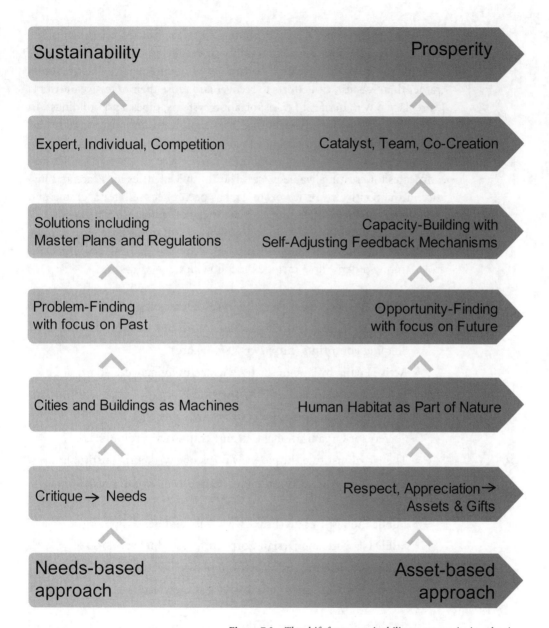

Figure 7.3 The shift from sustainability to prosperity in urbanism

In industry, we are finally beginning to see a shift from built-in obsolescence to durability and endurability. In environmental and infrastructure planning, wastewater and stormwater are being regarded as resources rather than wastes, with efforts to recover and reuse their excessive nutrients to replace raw materials in transportation systems, pipes, and buildings.[3] In research generally, we are benefiting from significant inroads toward bridging disciplines while also bridging theory and practice.

Numerous community organizations have become powerful allies and advocates for creating livable places. The Youth Ministries for Peace and Justice in the South Bronx, for example, has been effectively reimagining and rebuilding the Bronx River through a strategy of "transforming people, systems, and infrastructure" (http://ympj.org/about.html#strategy). Rapidly proliferating border-crossing organizations are also playing an important role. Among others, these include the following:

- Center for Ecoliteracy (http://www.ecoliteracy.org)[4]
- Design for Health (http://www.designforhealth.net)[5]
- Shaping Footprints (http://www.sfpinc.org)[6]
- Active Living by Design (http://www.activelivingbydesign.org)[7]
- Project for Public Spaces (http://www.pps.org)
- Walkable Communities (http://www.walkable.org)
- Society for Organizational Learning (http://www.solonline.org)
- The Urbal Institute (http://www.turnstone.tv/theurbalinstitut.html)
- Project for Livable Communities (http://livablecommunities .wordpress.com/)
- Public Interest Design (http://www.publicinterestdesign.org)
- SEED Network and Design Corps (http://seednetwork.org)
- Public Architecture (http://www.publicarchitecture.org)
- Slow Cities Movement (http://www.cittaslow.net)

This shift is also evident in the training and practice of professional urbanists. Many schools are moving away from the "crit" (critique), which points out deficits in students' work, to "conversations," in which students and teachers engage in a two-way learning process characterized by "appreciative inquiry" (Cooperrider and Whitney 2005; also see chapter 3, note 3.

For planning curricula, Sandercock (2003, 76) recommends conveying "at least six different ways of knowing, in addition to what is usually taught," including "knowing through dialogue; from experience; through seeking out local knowledge of the specific and concrete; through learning to read symbolic, non-verbal evidence; through contemplation; and through action-planning."

John Landis describes the shift in planning thought as follows:

> Planning is in the midst of a major paradigm change. . . . Planning's first paradigm, which ran in the U.S. from the turn of the 20th century until the early 1970s, was all about plan-making and regulation: Community plans were developed to lay out future land use and infrastructure patterns, and accompanying land use regulations—typically subdivision controls and zoning—were adopted as implementation tools. Planning's second paradigm, which rose out of the environmental movement during the 1970s, was all about making the planning process more participatory; and then, beginning in the 1980s, more cognizant of uneven power relationships. . . . The new planning paradigm, call it Planning 3.0, will be all about measuring outcomes and *developing implementation models that generate successful outcomes.* . . . Planning 3.0 will be instantaneous in speed, collaborative in nature, and global in scope. . . . In the realm of urban design, *Planning 3.0 will leave dogmatic labels behind, take on an international bent, and focus on how people actually use public and private spaces, and how they add to the urban livability.* (Landis 2011, emphasis added)[8]

According to Jonathan Barnett (2011, 208): "What is needed now is not a new all-purpose city-design concept, but new ways of integrating city design with the process of economic and social change and the need for a sustainable relationship with nature."

Practitioners of planning, urban design, architecture, and landscape architecture at the forefront of this shift tend to regard human habitat as part of nature, rather than a machine for living. They aspire to local and global prosperity, rather than aiming principally for power, prestige, and profits.

Many of these practitioners are developing and implementing important tools for creative engagement that have been unleashed by interactive, ubiquitous mobile technologies (Scearce 2011, Leadbeater 2008, Onuma 2010). The goal is to render the design and planning process more inclusive, accountable, and effective, deeply inflecting the product. For instance, the Campaign for Community-Based Planning produced the document "Planning for All New Yorkers" to provide communities with resources to plan their futures and inform future efforts at reforming New York's land use process (Municipal Arts Society Planning Center 2011). The Detroit Collaborative Design Center, under the leadership of Dan Pitera, uses a "Roaming Table" that can be set up anywhere to provide information and have one-on-one conversations as well as Twitter Town Halls and other unique engagement tools. Another example is the Onuma System (see the BIMStorm and Onuma System case study in chapter 4). Thanks to the proliferation of conversations facilitated by new technologies, we are shifting from a culture organized primarily around production and consumption to a culture of innovation (Leadbeater 2008).

Through this shift, an evolved contextualism has been emerging whereby geography, history, culture, experiential qualities, and post-occupancy evaluations become primary generators of form. The older contextualism, which asked new buildings to be harmonious with surroundings rather than scream "look at me," particularly en masse, has also taken stronger root. As Rem Koolhaas (2010, 68) recently declared: "An icon may be individually plausible, but . . . collectively they form an ultimately counterproductive and self-cancelling kind of landscape. So that is out." Visual representations express this evolved contextualism, a welcome departure from the conventional pristine architectural rendering devoid of people, often from a bird's-eye view as though the viewer is peering down upon a model.

Sustainability indicators are also evolving to be more inclusive, adaptive, and dynamic. One example is the Sustainable Built Environment Tool, or SuBET©, also described as Integral Indicators, developed by Husam Al-Waer with Derek Clements-Croome and Hilson Moran Consulting Engineers (Al-Waer and Hilson Moran 2010). These harbingers and enablers of good urbanism are a welcome improvement over the indicators that fail to adequately acknowledge site, cultural specificity, or the temporal dimension.

Just as complementary medicine looks at whole people, including their physical environment, a complementary urbanism would look at the whole environment, including people. Complementary urbanism has been emerging around the world parallel to rapidly proliferating complementary currencies, such as travel miles, time banking, and local currencies. Similar to complementary currencies, it complements what is already there rather than attempting to replace it or compete with it. In the case of urbanism, what is already there may include existing buildings and infrastructure, market economies, and cultural traditions, as well as theories about which approach may be optimal. In the same way that complementary currencies liberate people from the pyramidal global economy's concentration of power and control along with its excesses and predatory behaviors (Collective Intelligence Research Institute 2012), a complementary urbanism is not bound to the pyramidal urban development process and can benefit from the innovation, dynamism, and resilience allowed by leveraging collective intelligence. Hence, a complementary urbanism allows for wider input.

Writing in 1930 amid the economic and social upheavals of the Great Depression, economist John Maynard Keynes presaged the current realignment:

> I look forward . . . to the greatest change which has ever occurred in the material environment of life for human beings in the aggregate. But, of course, it will all happen gradually. . . . The course of affairs will simply be that there will be ever larger and larger classes and groups of people from whom problems of economic necessity have been practically removed. The critical difference will be realized when this condition has become so general that the nature of one's duty to one's neighbor is changed. For it will remain reasonable to be economically purposive for others after it has ceased to be reasonable for oneself. . . . *We shall once more value ends above means and prefer the good to the useful.* (Keynes 1963, 373, emphasis added)

In the meantime, he writes, "for at least another hundred years we must pretend to ourselves and to everyone that fair is foul and foul is fair; for foul is useful and fair is not. Avarice and usury and precaution must be our gods for a little longer still. For only they can lead us out of the tunnel of economic necessity into daylight" (Keynes 1963, 373).

Moving toward the hundred-year point marked by Keynes's prophetic remarks, the upward spiral toward prosperity is becoming apparent at all scales, from the wastebasket to the watershed. As William McDonough and Michael Braungart (2003) maintain: "We are increasingly able to design products and places that support life, that create footprints to delight in rather than lament. . . . Instead of asking, 'How do I meet today's environmental standards, designers are asking 'How might I create more habitat, more health, more clean water, more prosperity, more delight?'" McDonough (2011) contends: "We're designing forth into a world of abundance. . . . We don't see a world of limits."

The shift toward prosperity in urbanism is part of what Paul Hawken described several years ago as a worldwide "movement with no name" that will prevail because it is based not on ideology but on the identification of what is humane, behaving like an immune system to heal social and urban malaise (Hawken 2007). Though it may have no name, some keywords and characteristics of the new paradigm are:

Figure 7.4   Place

Figure 7.5   Process

Figure 7.6 Social Relations

Partnering
Alliances
Coalitions Participatory
Collaboration
SocialRelations
Co-working/CollaborativeWorkspaces
Networking Teamwork Collectives

Figure 7.7 Activities and Outcomes

SituatedCognition
SocialMedia
MultidisciplinaryPractices
ServiceLearning
TextingAndMalking
Multilogue
Infotainment
ActivitiesAndOutcomes
CommunityBasedResearch
VirtualOffices
Re-engineering
CampusWithoutWalls
InternetStalking
Transdisciplinarity
SocialEmbeddedness
ReturnToApprenticeships
Browsing/SurfingTheInternet

Figure 7.8 Technology Categories

TelefusionAndNarrowcasting

MobileInternet NotebookComputers E-mail

IntegratedServicesDigitalNetwork

Mobile CollaborativeSoftware

Multimedia E-commerce/M-commerce PDA

TechnologyCategories

WirelessWeb InstructionalManagement Networking

IntegratedCommunicationMix

DistanceLearning

InteractiveCableTV

Audio/VideoConferencing

Figure 7.9 Ways of Describing It

Jambalaya Fusion R/urbalism-Rural+Urban

WaysOfDescribingIt Hybridity

Hip-hopCulture

ExperienceEconomy

CongestionAndContamination

Figure 7.10 Values/Interests

Biodiversity

TheExtraordinaryInTheOrdinary

SpiritualityAndDepthfulness

FullnessInEmptiness

Edges/Zones/Periphery

Borders/Borderlands/TheMiddleLandscape

TheMarvelousInTheMundane

Values/Interests

Authenticity

Efficiency

SynergyAndInterdependence

Gifts/Abundance/Plenitude

OutsideIsTheNewInside

SimplicityWithinComplexity

ResilienceAndEndurance

Stewardship/Leadership/Responsibility

SlownessWithinAcceleration

GreenIsTheNewBlack

SincerityInContrastToIronyAndSarcasm

8 | Sideways Urbanism: Rotating the Pyramid

*What's beginning to emerge is very different from what's
gone before: we can't entirely eliminate things like hierarchy,
but what's coming may have no tops or bottoms, or even a
name.*

—James Hillman (2011)

*Today it is valuable to recognize that we have a unique
opportunity to reconsider the core of the disciplines that help
us think about the phenomenon of the urban.*

—Mohsen Mostafavi (2010, 5)

THOMAS CAMPANELLA RECENTLY TOUCHED A NERVE in the planning field by expos-
ing a concern that it had become a "trivial profession" (Campanella 2011).

Asking "How did a profession that roared to life with grand ambitions become such a mouse?" Campanella (2011) posed this challenge:

> How can we cultivate in planners the kind of visionary think-
> ing that once characterized the profession? How can we ensure
> that the idealism of our students is not extinguished as they
> move into practice? How can we transform planners into big-
> picture thinkers with the courage to imagine alternatives to the
> status quo, and equipped with the skills and the moxie to lead
> the recovery of American infrastructure and put the nation
> on a greener, more sustainable path? . . . We have become a
> caretaker profession—reactive rather than proactive, correc-
> tive instead of preemptive, rule bound and hamstrung and
> anything but visionary. If we lived in Nirvana, this would be
> fine. But we don't. We are entering the uncharted waters of
> global urbanization on a scale never seen. And we are not in
> the wheelhouse, let alone steering the ship. We may not even
> be on board.

Several years ago, sociologist Nathan Glazer (2007, 270) made a similar observation:

> Most observers of the city today would agree that the image
> of the planner in the public mind is not very defined or com-
> pelling, indeed rather dim. City planning, large-scale planning
> in general, is not in high repute these days, . . . It is clear the
> dominant element in the image of the planner is no longer that
> of the reformer, the bringer of hope, which is what the image
> of the city planner, I believe, used to be. . . . The planner today
> knows many details of many programs and the arguments
> that support one or another, but larger visions are beyond his
> responsibility. . . . And as a corollary, we do not normally think
> of calling in the professional planner when we consider today
> what has gone wrong with the city and suburb, and what can be
> done about it. These days we call him in to help with the details.

More than a decade prior, James Howard Kunstler (1993) queried simply: "Does the modern profession called urban planning have anything to do with making good places anymore?"

What about architects and urban designers? About architects, Glazer (2007, 290) declared: "The long history of the relationship of architects to the design of cities seems to have come to an end, or at least a temporary stop. Architects no longer design cities, and they are not being asked to. A relationship between architects and the design of cities that goes back to the Renaissance and perhaps before, and continued through the American City Beautiful movement and through early modernism, is for the moment in suspension."

Regarding urban designers, Alex Krieger (2009, 127) registered a parallel lament:

> The heroic form-giving tradition may be in decline. After all, the twentieth century witnessed immense urban harm caused by those who offered a singular or universal idea of what a city is, or what urbanization should produce. But our cultural observers remind us that pragmatism and technique cannot be a sufficient substitute, nor can design professionals be mere absorbers of public opinion waiting for consensus to build. One must think and offer ideas as well. . . . But such deliverers of bold saber strokes (to borrow a phrase from Gideon) are rarer today than they were at the turn of the 20th century, or we heed their visions less often.

With those trained to design cities not playing principal roles, the job has largely defaulted to private developers in negotiation with city councils and development review boards. What precipitated the turn of events?

When Daniel Burnham sang the praises of big plans a century ago, it was a period of rapid urban growth, and the creation of numerous city plans and visions ensued over the next half century. With the widely acknowledged failure of modern urbanism, however, confusion and a credibility crisis considerably diminished such visioning. The shortcomings of modern urbanism owed to both product and process, the *what* as well as the *how*. With regard to product (the what), modern urbanism's principal banes were the separation of functions, the death of the street, and the reliance on the automobile. In terms of process (the how), problems inhered in imposing plans on places without meaningful community engagement and with disregard for the existing built and natural landscapes, history, and culture. In the wake of modern urbanism's demise, numerous "open society" and participatory efforts emerged that avoided the heavy hand but proved largely unsatisfactory in terms of improving places.

The first shortcoming (product) has been ably addressed since then by the converging prescriptions for good urbanism described in the introduction.[1] The second one (process), however, has been largely evaded, severely impairing the professions of planning and urban design. Retreating from addressing core issues, these professions deflected attention to more narrow pursuits, technological preoccupations, and turf wars (battling urbanisms rather than good urbanism, competing for commissions, and so forth). Needless to say, prescribing good urbanism without the ability to heed such prescriptions cannot fully repair the shortcomings of modern urbanism, likely explaining the ongoing lament about the paucity of bold plans ever since the failure of modern urbanism.

Happily, as described in this book, another kind of visionary planning and urban design has been on the rise that responds to both shortcomings. This new breed understands the power of co-creation and how it can sharpen other tools of the trade. Throughout history, all the way through modern urbanism, visionary planning and urban design were essentially top-down. The reaction since the 1960s was emphatically bottom-up. Since then, diluted versions of both have characterized most efforts with largely mixed or underwhelming results.

Neither top-down nor bottom-up, the most recent exemplary practices, as illustrated by many of the case studies in this book, might be characterized as *sideways urbanism*. This approach can be initiated by anyone—political leaders, planners, architects, urban designers, landscape architects, artists, developers, philanthropic organizations, cultural institutions, universities, or interested community members.[2] It begins with an idea hatched by one or more people who quickly invite all stakeholders to refine and realize the vision. In the process, these practices establish an entity to oversee and monitor the project along with enabling policy to facilitate its implementation and allow others to easily replicate it.

Sideways (or lateral) urbanism follows the Path toward Prosperity (see chapter 2) or variations thereof.[3] With an eye to enhancing places for people, these efforts turn the pyramid on its side. Combining the "hierarchy of needs" with the "hierarchy of assets," this rotated pyramid might look something like figure 8.1 (plate 16).

With Fuels (energy sources) and Tools (knowledge and technology), people come up with ideas, work collaboratively with others to develop them, and rally the resources necessary for implementation. Manifesting ideas and benefiting from their impacts satisfies physiological, safety, social, and esteem needs, which are, in fact, inextricable, not piled neatly one atop the other.

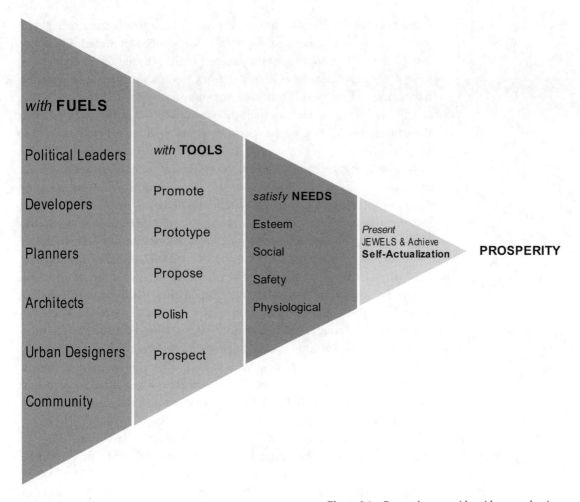

Figure 8.1 Prosperity pyramid: a sideways urbanism

Building on existing strengths of places and communities, Jewels are crafted that contribute to self-actualization.

Whereas the onus previously was on the decision makers at the top of the traditional organization chart, now the bulk of the work is done before reaching them. *Instead of diminishing their power, however, this approach actually empowers them more* because they have enabled the process to occur, or at least sanctioned it, and through co-creation, the process delivers a product that has been polished by the interested parties who have already taken ownership of the project, invested in making it happen, and will feel proud of it when it does. Indeed, so much has already been accomplished by the time it reaches the final decision makers that this process greatly reduces the huge investment typically required to get an idea approved, allocate resources to build it, and obtain support of the general public. Without this process, these steps are unreliable at best. With it, the project has actually already started happening and the simple rubber stamp of decision makers, now at the side as true civil servants, ensures their popularity and continued support from the community. Plus, they can claim bragging rights to a highly successful project in their city or town.

While everyone can contribute to restoring health and well-being to our places, as described throughout this book, professional urbanists play a special role. Planners, architects, urban designers, and landscape architects contribute by providing their vast respective expertise, experience, and understanding of how best to extend the various traditions of city building: the humanist, landscape ecology, systems, and form-making avant-garde. Professional urbanists can also provide guidance to and along the path toward prosperity, assisting all to engage in ongoing positive transformation. As architectural philosopher Karsten Harries (1998, 264) reminds, professional urbanists should be vigilant not to separate intuition and ethics from craft/technology. Counterintuitively, and learning from the most successful contemporary practices, professionals expand their influence and impact to the extent they work with others. The more they recognize and engage stakeholders at all levels, the better their proposals and the more consistently they are realized.

Urbanists also contribute by connecting with others from different fields. While professional and disciplinary boundaries divide the world into categories that may inoculate from having to deal with the "slash" where things come together, it is in fact these border regions that are often the most important to tend (Ellin 2006, 133–34). Finally, professional urbanists can contribute by connecting with the places and communities where they live and work.

Philosopher Lawrence Haworth, author of *The Good City*, asserted back in the 1960s that the goal of planners should be to create good places for people, and he was critical of those who were deciding "what would be good for people to do, and then [arranging] for the facilities by which they might be made to do those things" (Haworth 1965).[4] After several dark decades, the profession is now spiraling back up. As Cliff Ellis (2005, 144) maintains: "The planning profession is being offered a golden opportunity to finally 'get it right' with respect to the design of cities and regions, as well as to become linked in the public mind with accomplishments of the highest order." But, Ellis notes, "this opportunity will be wasted if planners are not trained to handle physical planning issues with confidence, subtlety, and intelligence; to distinguish good places from bad or mediocre ones; to collaborate successfully with our allied professions in design and engineering; and to educate a broad public about alternatives to the status quo" (2005, 144).[5] Campanella's own antidote for making planners more visionary and influential is to cram more material than possible into their training so they become masters of all trades.[6] He contends: "Planners today need not a close-up lens or a wide-angle lens but a wide-angle zoom lens" (Campanella 2011).

While it is important for planners to understand the big picture, it is also important to work effectively in teams. Rather than colonize related fields, planners could deepen their impact by building on existing strengths. These include the ability to work at multiple scales simultaneously—seeing "the world in a grain of sand" and vice versa—while also being "situationalists" by distinguishing among mandates to employ appropriate techniques and strategies.[7] The planning toolkit also includes collaborating, facilitating, benchmarking, assessing impacts, imagining alternatives, community building, consensus building, listening, communicating, storytelling, stewarding, educating, and placemaking.

By applying these skills along the Path toward Prosperity, the goal of transforming "planners into big-picture thinkers with the courage to imagine alternatives to the status quo" (Campanella 2011) could be achieved. This would contribute "to recover the creative dynamic of the planning project," as recommended by planning theorist Patsy Healey (2006, 336–37). It would perhaps offer the "new qualities of planning imagination," including an "epistemology of multiplicity," for which Leonie Sandercock eloquently appeals (2003, 3, 76). As innovators and leaders, planners could thereby fulfill what Lewis Mumford described long ago as "the promise of planning." In a similar vein, urban designers[8], architects, and landscape architects could also channel their capacities toward more impactful ends. As Joan Busquets (Busquets and Correa 2007, 15) remarks: "Men and women as social beings are creating new forms of 'urbanness', and it falls to us to interpret them and create processes and urban forms for these new conditions."

In addition to connecting with other fields through practice, professional urbanists can also bridge the divides through research. While some important work has been linking people and place, most notably addressing the correlation between walkable cities and obesity along with other aspects of public health (Ewing et al. 2006, Frumkin, Frank, and Jackson 2004, Corburn 2009, Dannenberg, Frumkin, and Jackson 2011, Forsyth and Richardson 2011), much more can be done. This kind of work is not encouraged, however, when academics are confined to silos that are disconnected from related fields and subject to a reward system that privileges research read by a handful of others over public scholarship or practical applications. The passion that drove academics to their chosen fields is often stifled or extinguished, diminishing the quality of their work, their potential impact, and their ability to inspire and mentor future generations.

So as not to squander precious intellectual capital, universities are starting to adjust the reward system to recognize impactful work.[9] A frontrunner of this movement, President Michael Crow of Arizona State University advocates "socially embedded" and "outcome-oriented" research, declaring: "We must no longer allow our universities to remain aloof from their communities. . . . It is time for universities to recognize their moral responsibilities, both for the knowledge they produce and to the communities in which they exist. . . . We must encourage intellectual fusion and create transdisciplinary knowledge that solves real-world problems, and not simply isolate ourselves to produce knowledge for the sake of knowledge itself" (Crow 2007). This groundswell of support for engaged scholarship is long overdue and duly welcome, enabling the dedication of vast human and institutional resources to positive transformation on the local, national, and global scales.

9 | Conclusion

GOOD URBANISTS MAY BE CIVIC LEADERS, place-healers, creative entrepreneurs (who contribute unique local businesses), or entrepreneurial creatives (artists). Good urbanists can also be connectors, mavens (researchers), and salespersons (advocates), the three capacities required for real transformation, according to Malcolm Gladwell in *The Tipping Point* (2000).

Just as a good manager builds on the existing strengths of an organization, good urbanists build on what is already there. Whether professional urbanists or anyone else interested in contributing to improve the places we live, they begin by uncovering individual hunches and identifying assets. Then they engage others to consider how best to leverage these assets, envision best possibilities, and manifest these.

Good urbanism builds on what is integral to people and locales—their *prima materia* or DNA—rather than focusing on deficits and problems. Good urbanism enhances places by leveraging these existing conditions, including natural landscapes, history, culture, buildings, neighborhoods, businesses, cultural institutions, schools, and the talents, ideas, and skills of community members. In this way, good urbanism contributes to supporting existing local businesses and creating incentives for new ones while also providing an attractive place for national and global businesses to establish themselves. It builds on cultural assets, supporting the rich diversity of our communities, including historic buildings and districts, expressive arts and culture, and the wide range of creativity and expertise in any given place. And, it showcases environmental assets, along with our ability to reclaim and enhance them, often featuring connected public space systems and integrating more nature into the city. In the process, a generative and dynamic self-adjusting feedback mechanism is set into motion, enabling communities to build creatively on their strengths in an ongoing fashion.

While forward-looking, good urbanism also honors and carries on traditions, rather than mimicking history. For instance, it may honor Detroit's tradition of being innovative, rather than attempting to continue its history of producing cars. Good urbanism may develop and blend several traditions simultaneously rather than choosing just one.

Recurrent themes of good urbanism are *slow*, *flow*, *low*, and *local*. Placing a brake on rapid change and the havoc it can wreak, slowness is apparent in the Slow City (http://www.cittaslow.org) and Slow Food (http://www.slowfood.com) movements, recalling Mae West's observation that "anything worth doing is worth doing slowly." Slowness is also apparent in appeals for incremental urbanism (Alexander et al. 1987, Attoe and Logan 1989, Kemmis 1995). The evolved contextualism of good urbanism finds existing *flows*, honors them, and/or unblocks them to clear physical as well as social blockages. The most simple, elegant, and efficient urban design solutions are often *low*-impact and *low*-tech—for instance, the use of swales, cisterns, and gray water instead of sewers and municipal water, along with urban agriculture replacing nonproductive right-of-ways, grass lawns, and the purchase of produce from grocery stores. And, the mantra of the moment is grow, eat, shop, hire, incubate (ideas, technologies, and businesses), and generate (energy) *local* (McKibben 2007) (figure 9.1).

In sum, good urbanism aims to raise quality of life by enhancing "quality of place." To achieve this, it brings people together to have conversations that paint a vision of what could be and energize all to implement the vision. Rather than use fear and control, good urbanism applies inspiration and modeling. Good urbanism transmutes the greatest problems into the greatest solutions by revealing blessings that may be disguised and by making virtue of necessity.

Good urbanism follows the Path toward Prosperity by taking six steps: prospect, polish, propose, prototype, promote, and present. It engages in urban acupuncture by removing blockages in "urban meridians," thereby

Figure 9.1 "How local can you go?" at Whole Foods in Salt Lake City, Utah (Credit: Nan Ellin)

liberating the life force of a city and bringing urban and economic revitalization. Good urbanism thus restores connections that have been severed over the past century between body and soul, between people and nature, and among people.

The strength and resilience of relationships and communities rely on trust, but trust eroded with the urban fragmentation of the second half of the twentieth century, allowing an "architecture of fear" to occupy the void (Ellin 1997). Good urbanism fosters community by cultivating relationships through a process that engages and builds mutually supportive networks of people. The trust on which relationships and communities rely ensues.

Good urbanism combines strategy with serendipity. In contrast to popular efforts to "conspire with reality," good urbanism is not principally tactical. The tactical approach may be that of the spy or double agent fulfilling an agenda, which might be covert and self-serving. Or, it may be that of the guerilla community builder aiming to make specific interventions, usually in the guerilla's own neighborhood, skirting political processes (Lydon et al. 2011). While the tactical approach is often cynical, and sometimes passive-aggressive, good urbanism aims clearly and idealistically to enhance places for all people. It invests in planning and designing the process, reaping handsome returns: a successful product. Both process and product contribute to create synergies, efficiencies, and relationships.

Good urbanism is generative and proactive, rather than reactive. It moves beyond the professional as *deus ex machina*, *auteur*, or micromanager and beyond competition for the 3 Ps: power, prestige, and profits. It is not top-down, but nor is it bottom-up. It is a sideways urbanism, with segments of decision makers, urban design professionals, and communities working side by side toward mutually beneficial ends. Good urbanism invites professional urbanists and stakeholders to participate, welcomes them when they do, and partners with them to bring ideas to life.

Good urbanism generates places that are livable and lovable, places where people feel connected with themselves, others, nature, locales, the sacred, the past, and the future. Good urbanism envisions best possibilities and rallies resources to realize them, in a world that needs these now more than ever. It does this by rendering the latent manifest and the improbable inevitable.

Good urbanism is increasingly apparent and possible everywhere.

Are you a good urbanist?

Appendix A: Themes/Features of Good Urbanism

- Slow
- Flow
- Low
- Local
- Nature in the city
- Connected open space systems
- Network model for cities and regions
- Adaptive reuse: buildings and infrastructure
- Transit-oriented development
- Walkability and bikeability
- Creative entrepreneurship
- Entrepreneurial creativity
- Collaborative professional teams with a range of expertise
- Co-creation with stakeholders, sometimes using mobile interactive technologies and social media
- Conversations about urbanism that take place online, in print media, on radio and TV, in salons, with neighborhood associations, and in public spaces and "third places" (Oldenberg 2007).

Table A.1: Case Study Themes

Projects	Slow	Flow	Low	Local	Nature in the City	Connected Open Space Systems	Network Model for Cities and Regions	Adaptive Reuse: Buildings and Infrastructure	Transit-Oriented Development	Walkability and Bikeability	Creative Entrepreneurship	Entrepreneurial Creativity	Collaborative Teams	Co-Creation with Stakeholders	Community Engagement	Conversations about Urbanism
The High Line New York City, NY		✔		✔	✔	✔		✔		✔		✔	✔	✔	✔	✔
Canalscape Phoenix Metropolitan Region		✔	✔	✔	✔	✔	✔	✔	✔	✔	✔	✔	✔	✔	✔	✔
Civic Center Various	✔		✔	✔				✔			✔	✔	✔	✔	✔	✔
Envision Utah Utah	✔	✔	✔	✔	✔	✔	✔		✔	✔			✔	✔	✔	✔
BIMstorm and the Onuma System Anywhere		✔				✔	✔						✔	✔	✔	✔
Open Space Seattle 2100 Seattle Metropolitan Region		✔	✔	✔	✔	✔	✔	✔		✔			✔	✔	✔	✔
The CEDAR Approach Hooper, UT	✔	✔	✔	✔	✔	✔							✔	✔		✔
University of Arkansas Community Design Center Arkansas	✔	✔	✔	✔	✔	✔		✔	✔	✔			✔	✔	✔	
Sunrise Park Charlottesville, VA				✔	✔	✔		✔		✔			✔	✔	✔	✔
Groundwork Ballpark District of Minneapolis, MN		✔		✔	✔	✔		✔	✔	✔		✔	✔	✔	✔	✔

Appendix B: Good Urbanism Is . . .

Asset-Based

Good urbanism focuses on revealing and celebrating what already exists and drawing inspiration from it. Good urbanism enhances places by leveraging these assets, which include natural landscapes, history, culture, buildings, neighborhoods, businesses, cultural institutions, schools, and the talents, ideas, and skills of community members. Good communication about urbanism ("construing construction") similarly begins with an appreciation for existing assets, in contrast to the modernist genre of criticism.

Complementary

Just as complementary medicine looks at whole people, including their physical environment, complementary urbanism looks at the whole environment, including people. Similar to complementary currencies—such as travel miles, time banking, and local currencies—good urbanism complements what is already there rather than attempting to replace or compete with it. Good urbanism protects what is valued, enhances what may be underperforming, and then builds on this *tabula plena* (full slate) rather than a *tabula rasa* (erased slate).

Inclusive and Idealistic

Good urbanism aims to effect real change and create prosperous places where people can live prosperous lives. Good urbanism is *by all* (co-creative) and *for all.* It invites a wide range of professionals and stakeholders to participate, welcomes them when they do, and partners with them to bring ideas to life. Good urbanism is neither top-down nor bottom-up. It is a sideways urbanism, with segments of decision makers, urban design professionals, and communities working side by side toward mutually beneficial ends. Good urbanism measures its success in terms of quality of life, not by the 3 P's: power, profit, and prestige.

Skilled and Professional

While inclusive, good urbanism also relies on the expertise and experience of professional urbanists—architects, planners, urban designers, and landscape architects—often working in multidisciplinary teams. In addition to providing technical skills, professional urbanists bring an understanding of which city-building traditions may be appropriate for any given situations—the humanist, landscape ecology, systems, and form-making avant-garde—and can offer guidance to and along the path toward prosperity. Professional good urbanists plan and design the process, sharpening other tools of the trade and lending to a successful product.

Proactive and Pragmatic

Good urbanism is not principally tactical, but instead combines strategy with serendipity. While forward-looking, good urbanism honors and carries on traditions rather than mimicking history. Good urbanism may develop and blend several traditions simultaneously rather than choosing just one. Good urbanism envisions best possibilities and rallies support and resources to realize them.

A Process as Well as a Product

Good urbanism describes an approach to enhancing the health and vitality of places for people as well as the resultant places themselves.

Generative and Integrative

The process and product of good urbanism create synergies, efficiencies, and relationships. Good urbanism sets a generative and dynamic self-adjusting feedback mechanism into motion, enabling communities to build creatively on their strengths in an ongoing fashion.

Transformative

Good urbanism can transmute problems into opportunities by revealing blessings that may be disguised and making virtue of necessity. Moving beyond sustainability to prosperity, good urbanism envisions and realizes better futures in a world that needs them now more than ever.

Notes

Chapter 1. Introduction

1. Research undertaken by Zeynep Toker and Henrik Minassians (2011) draws a similar conclusion.

2. Earlier versions include Ebenezer Howard's Garden Cities, the "neighborhood unit" of Clarence Perry, the "cellular city" of Lewis Mumford, Pedestrian Pockets (Kelbaugh 1996), and Transit-Oriented Developments.

3. Ray Oldenburg describes these informal public gathering places as the "third place," after home and work (2007).

4. See Morrish and Brown (1993) and Berrizbeitia and Pollak (1999).

5. For instance, Volkswagen sponsors the "fun theory" (http://thefuntheory.com/), "dedicated to the thought that something as simple as fun is the easiest way to change people's behaviour for the better."

6. The work of Jan Gehl (2010, 2011) has contributed greatly to this discussion regarding urban design. For design generally, *Metropolis* magazine identified "ten criteria for evaluating design arguments today, in the troubled economic, ecological, and political climate of the early 21st century" (Hall 2009), proclaiming that "good design" is sustainable, accessible, functional, well made, emotionally resonant, enduring, socially beneficial, beautiful, ergonomic, and affordable (ibid).

7. Brenda Scheer phrases the question in the following way, the "we" referring specifically to urban designers: "We know how to design cities. . . . So why is it that for every much-heralded 50-acre new urbanism gesture, there are literally thousands of acres of new strip malls, gas stations, apartment complexes, office parks, subdivisions, and big box stores. Multiscreen theaters, convention centers, soccer stadiums, airports, and shopping malls all resist the good urbanism lessons. . . . What it is that we don't understand that confounds our attempts to change this ubiquitous landscape?" (Scheer 2010, 1).

8. This inquiry into good urbanism recalls the Museum of Modern Art's series of four exhibitions in the 1950s and 1960s called "What Is Good Design?" and the 2011 retrospective "What Was Good Design? 1944–56."

Chapter 2. Urban Desiderata: A Path toward Prosperity

1. Love for a place has been described as "topophilia" (Bachelard 1994, Tuan 1990).

2. The goal of creating places that are not only livable, but also lovable, has been addressed in Ellin 2009, 2010a, and 2012. On a related theme, Steve Mouzon speaks of the importance of lovable buildings; see, for example, http://www.originalgreen.org/foundations/lovable/.

3. John Forester (1989) advocates this when he speaks of knowledge emerging from discourse and the importance of "self-reflection."

4. This step contributes to correcting the tendency to erase our personal histories and preferences. Leonie Sandercock (2003, 200) describes this tendency with regard to planning students: "Students have been constituted as targets for a one-directional flow of skills and knowledge, without the interference of gender, race, class, ethnicity, or sexual orientation; and they have been expected to sever the connections between personal and professional worlds as they learn to subordinate their other identities to the task of becoming a professional."

5. The literature on community engagement is extensive; see, for example, Faga 2006, Healey 2006, and many more.

Chapter 3. The Tao of Urbanism: Rendering the Latent Manifest and the Possible Inevitable

1. According to anthropologist Angeles Arrien (1993).

2. John McKnight and Peter Block elaborate: "A scarcity mindset and its consequence, competition, develop political effects. We become willing to give up more and more autonomy. We remain ignorant of knowing what inherent and natural gifts surround us. We lose touch with our neighbors and do not assemble or associate. All the things we so believe in are not taken from us; we give them away freely" (McKnight and Block 2010, 110).

3. The approach of Appreciative Inquiry (AI), developed for organization management, "involves systematic discovery of what gives 'life' to a living system when it is most alive, most effective, and most constructively capable in economic, ecological, and human terms. AI involves, in a central way, the art and practice of asking questions that strengthen a system's capacity to apprehend, anticipate, and heighten positive

potential. . . . AI deliberately, in everything it does, seeks to work from accounts of this 'positive change core'—and it assumes that every living system has many untapped and rich and inspiring accounts of the positive. Link the energy of this core directly to any change agenda and changes never thought possible are suddenly and democratically mobilized" (Cooperrider and Whitney 2005). Appreciative Inquiry (AI) applies a "4-D" cycle to organizational management: Discover, Dream, Design, and Deliver. A good summary of AI by Richard Seel can be found at http://www .new-paradigm.co.uk/introduction_to_ai.htm.

4. For designer Jim Fournier, the process of *polishing* and *proposing* "feels as if one is discovering a solution, which was already present in potential and had to be teased out, discovered, in order to be brought into manifestation. It is very much an experience of humility and awe rather than intellectual triumph and control" (Fournier 1999).

5. William McDonough and Michael Braungart have developed a similar formulation, suggesting we start with values (asking what we hold dear), then move to principles (their Hannover Principles), and then establish goals, strategies, tactics, and metrics. Instead, most practices begin with metrics and go backward to propose tactics, strategies, and goals, but never get to principles and values (McDonough and Braungart 2003, McDonough 2011).

6. The Rudy Bruner Award for Urban Excellence, awarded biennially since 1987, has celebrated such projects in the United States: "They are born through processes of transformation—the renewal of something old, or the creation of something new that resonates in the history of community life. . . . An excellent urban place involves the interplay of process, place and values." (Rudy Bruner Foundation 2011).

7. Building relationships based on trust, this process generates human and social capital to advance the project for the benefit of all (Burt 2005, Fukuyama 1995, Putnam 2000, Blokland and Savage 2008).

8. The Rock Solid Foundation in Victoria, Canada, created the Trackside Gallery for this very purpose.

9. The Detroit Collaborative Design Center has proposed this.

10. Andre Viljoen and Katrin Bohn have advocated for "continuous productive urban landscape" (CPUL), interlinking multifunctional open space networks throughout cities that include urban agriculture, as well as other productive uses that complement and support the built environment (Viljoen 2005).

11. Andrés Edwards echoes this with a focus on environmental sustainability: "The transformation from sustainability to thriveability challenges us to expand our imaginations and create the future we want for ourselves and for future generations. Thriveability focuses on collaboration and abundance. . . . It encourages us to step away from the notion that we are separate from nature and instead see ourselves as an integral part of natural systems. . . . This thriveable attitude shifts away from scarcity, loss and volatility and toward abundance, prosperity and equanimity." To achieve this, he proposes the SPIRALS framework, whereby initiatives should be Scaleable, Place-making, Intergenerational, Resilient, Accessible, Life-affirming, and involve Self-care. (Edwards 2010).

12. Kennedy was paraphrasing a line from George Bernard Shaw's "Back to Methuselah."

13. This theme was further developed by Paul Hawken, Amory Lovins, and Hunter Lovins (1999).

14. The Banff Center Leadership Lab describes this approach as follows: "Design and leadership are fundamentally about actively creating the future rather than reacting to the present" (cited by Block 2008, 29).

Chapter 4. Co-Creation: From Egosystem to Ecosystem

1. Psychologist James Hillman describes this process as "seeing through," explained by Gail Thomas as follows: "First one must realize the idea, then allow the image to form, then proceed with the practical application. . . . If we get the image right, *it* (the image) actually moves the project" (in Hillman 2006, 12). Leonie Sandercock (2003, 204) describes the process: "This most ancient of arts begins with the sharing of stories, and moves toward the shaping of new collective stories."

2. Roberta Brandes Gratz (1994, 50, 105) provides excellent examples occurring in Savannah and the Bronx. In the case of revitalizing low-income neighborhoods, Jane Jacobs describes this as "unslumming" (1961, 353–80).

3. As Joan Busquets maintains: "Urbanism involves defining scenarios and ways of programming rather than the precise definition of potential yet unattainable realities that cannot advance beyond the formulation stage" (Busquets and Correa 2007, 14).

4. Christopher Alexander advocated such an approach, saying that every project must be expressed "as a vision which can be seen in the inner eye (literally). It must have this quality so strongly that it can be communicated to others, and felt by others, as a vision" (Alexander et al. 1987, 50).

5. The contraction "urbapreneur" was suggested by Jennifer J. Johnson and Sara Meess.

6. The "community indicator" field has grown significantly in recent years. As summarized by Maria Jackson: "The National Neighborhood Indicators Partnership is a collaborative effort involving the Urban Institute and several community indicator initiatives across the country to develop and use neighborhood-level information systems (http://www2.urban.org/nnip/). The Community Indicators Consortium is a 'learning network' for the development and use of community-level indicators (http://www.communityindicators.net/). The International Society for Quality of Life Studies is an international networking entity for people involved in quality of life studies (http://www.isqols.org/)" (Jackson et al, 2006). The Knight Foundation conducted a Gallup Poll called "Soul of the Community" (2008–10) (http://www.soulofthecommunity.org) and discovered a correlation between emotional attachment to places, passion for a place, loyalty to it, and gross domestic product. Emotional attachment to communities was found to be a function of social offerings, openness, aesthetics, education, basic services, leadership, economy,

emotional wellness, safety, social capital, and civic involvement (Knight Foundation 2011). A report by the Urban Institute measures the relationship between cultural vitality and community well-being (Jackson et al. 2006).

7. These projects range from "Envision Dixie" in southern Utah (home to Bryce Canyon and Zion National Park) to the "Bear Lake Valley Blueprint" for the area surrounding the lake that spans the Utah/Idaho border. "Envision Cache Valley" contemplates rapid population growth in northern Utah's agricultural base; "Blueprint Jordan River" sets a path toward embracing the river that runs through the heart of the Salt Lake Valley and into the Great Salt Lake; and "Wasatch Canyons Tomorrow" advances a vision and guiding principles for the future of the six canyons east of the Salt Lake Valley.

Chapter 5. Going with the Flow: The New Design with Nature

1. This term has been applied by Frampton (1999), Lerner (2003), de Solà-Morales (2004), Ellin (2006), and Koh and Beck-Koh (2007). Jaime Lerner (2010, 190) describes urban acupuncture, saying: "Strategic, timely interventions can release new energy and help consolidate it toward the desired goals [triggering] positive chain reactions, or 'spillovers' as [Jane] Jacobs described them, which will help to heal and enhance the whole system."

2. As defined by psychologist Mihaly Csikszentmihalyi (1990), flow is the intense experience situated between boredom and overstimulation characterized by immersion, awareness, and a sense of harmony, meaning, and purpose. While generally intended for enhancing individual performance such as playing sports, it is also useful to consider how places might be "in flow." For a discussion of applying the concept of flow to urbanism, see Ellin (2006, 5–7).

3. Attoe and Logan (1989, 45) describe this effect as "urban catalysis"—"a sequence of limited, achievable visions, each with the power to kindle and condition other achievable visions." These visions, they contend (ibid), "should be modest and incremental, but their impact should be substantial, in contrast to the large visions that have been the rule, with their minimal or catastrophic impact."

4. For a more in-depth discussion of integral urbanism, see Ellin 2006.

5. As Jane Jacobs (1961, 14) observed: "The ubiquitous principle . . . is the need of cities for a most intricate and close-grained diversity of uses that give each other constant mutual support, both economically and socially."

6. The reaction to modernism's focus on objects began a half century ago with the British Townscape Movement, which criticized the tendency to regard the city "as a kind of sculpture garden" (Jacobs and Appleyard 1987, 116) and emphasized the "art of relationship" (Cullen 1961) among all elements in the landscape. The reaction was also manifest in the "postwar humanist rebellion" (Tzonis and Lefaivre 1999) of Team

10. For instance, Shadrach Woods emphasized the importance of "human associations" and Alison and Peter Smithson advocated creating "the forms of habitat which can stimulate the development of human relations" and offered a list of relationships between different kinds of spaces at a 1955 CIAM gathering (Tzonis and Lefaivre 1999).

7. Aseem Inam (2011) advocates "transformative urbanism," whereby urbanists focus more on designing the process than the product in order to have transformative impacts by working as parts of teams, engaging communities, studying local construction techniques, mobilizing local resources, working with nonprofits, and transforming institutions.

8. Biologist Edward O. Wilson coined this term to describe a genetic preference for natural landscapes.

9. Benefits of integrating nature into human habitats are described by Wexler (1998), Thompson and Steiner (1997), Hough (1995), Condon (2010), Hellmund and Smith (2006), Register (2006), Farr (2007), and Beatley (2004).

10. Jim Fournier (1999) similarly points out that "there are fundamental chemical solutions in nature, which nature figured out millions of years ago and basically has not been able to improve upon ever since. It has instead continued to reuse them in ever changing permutations and ever more complex systems, but always based upon the same fundamental biochemical solutions which it devised millions of years ago."

11. As demonstrated by Ilya Prigogen in the 1960s.

12. Lewis Mumford started speaking of biotechnics in *Culture of Cities* (1938) and later expanded upon it (1967–70). The full context of the epigraph to this chapter is as follows:

> If we are to prevent megatechnics from further controlling and deforming every aspect of human culture, we shall be able to do so only with the aid of a radically different model derived directly, not from machines, but from living organisms and organic complexes. . . . Once an organic world picture is in the ascendant, the working aim of an economy of plenitude will be not to feed more human functions into the machine, but to develop further man's incalculable potentialities for self-actualization and self-transcendence, taking back into himself deliberately many of the activities he has too supinely surrendered into the mechanical system. . . . As opposed to [megatechnics], an organic system directs itself to qualitative richness, amplitude, spaciousness, free from quantitative pressure and crowding, since self-regulation, self-correction, and self-propulsion are as much an integral property of organisms as nutrition, reproduction, growth, and repair. Balance, wholeness, completeness, continuous interplay between inner and outer, the subjective and the objective aspects of existence are identifying characteristics of the organic model; and the general name for an economy based on such a model is an economy of plenitude." (Mumford 1967–70)

13. McDonough and Braungart (2003) contend: "Rather than aspire to a respectful co-existence with nature, we aim to celebrate human creativity and the abundance of the living earth with designs that create mutually beneficial relationships between people and the natural world."

14. Landscape urbanism, in particular, has contributed to creatively reclaiming brownfield sites and reinvigorating park design. It is less successful, however, when it fails to strengthen our connection with the land by neglecting social and experiential aspects of design—equity, access, comfort, and well-being. Also unfortunate has been a tendency to dismiss related fields—particularly planning and urban design—rather than build on their many contributions.

15. According to the Collective Intelligence Research Institute (2012), the implications are even more extensive: "The rise of Internet, of social media and collaborative technologies (*socialware* and *communityware*) catalyzes new social forms that were never observed before in human society. Although this transition is just beginning, it is perfectly noticeable that distributed and decentralized structures, built on plurality and very precise self-organizing modes, connected via online social media, are much more resilient, able to learn and adapt than anything that existed before. These new distributed structures are . . . an evolution of our species in regards to original collective intelligence (small group, village, tribe, team . . .) and pyramidal collective intelligence (medium and large organizations—governments, administrations, armies, enterprises, institutions, universities, religious orders, etc)."

16. Having addressed the 2002 United Nations Summit on Sustainable Development in Johannesburg, South Africa and spearheaded the Swaner Family Trust's dedication of prime real estate for the one-thousand-acre Swaner EcoCenter and Preserve in Summit County, Utah (http://www.swanerecocenter.org), Swaner is an eco-philanthropist who provides tools and consulting to help optimize what he views as the nation's critically shrinking open space.

17. For more details, see http://www.greeninfrastructuredesign.org/media/document/cedar-explained.pdf.

18. Peter Bednar recently left UACDC to develop the urban design division for Mada Spam Architects in Shanghai. UACDC's co-creators include the University of Arkansas Department of Biological and Agricultural Engineering, the Center for Business and Economic Research, Audubon Arkansas, and the Arkansas Forestry Commission.

19. "Vision California: Charting Our Future" (http://www.visioncalifornia.org/reports.php); "Envision Utah: The Quality Growth Strategy" (http://www.envisionutah.org/eu_about_eu_qualitygrowthstrategy_main.html); and "Oregon's Statewide Planning Goals & Guidelines" (http://www.oregon.gov/LCD/docs/goals/compilation_of_statewide_planning_goals.pdf?ga=t).

Chapter 6. The Art of Urbanism: A Practice Primer

1. The concept of MeSearch is adapted from Lynn Nelson (2004).

2. This approach loosely parallels Otto Scharmer's "Theory U," applying it specifically to enhancing quality of place. As Scharmer (2007, 467) maintains: "Learning from the past is based on the normal learning cycle (act, observe, reflect, plan, act), while learning from the future as it emerges is based on the process and practice of presencing (suspending, redirecting, letting go, letting come, envisioning, enacting, embodying)."

3. A graduate student who is also a professional planner, Dina Blaes, observed: "Our discussions around VIDA have informed my daily practice in ways I had never expected. The fundamental shift from articulating problems to identifying assets is more powerful than one might think. Seeking assets and the opportunities they represent is, individually, very mentally freeing. Instead of focusing on what part of the problem we may have missed, we are empowered to think beyond boundaries and structure. In a professional setting, the approach seems to put colleagues at ease and serves to draw them into a discussion or process. Rather than waiting to be blamed or formulating a defensive response, they engage and more readily join a discussion" (Blaes 2010). A former student, Colin Tetreault, who is currently sustainability advisor to the mayor of Phoenix, wrote that the VIDA process offered a "great template" for his job, which he describes as "translating the multiple 'languages' and finding a creative way to unleash the collective capacity of our city, region, and our citizens" (Tetreault 2012).

4. Weinstein (2009b) elaborates: "This problem is compounded by mass media coverage of star architects as spectacle-makers, icon producers—and rarely as relation-builders within the context of the community where their spectacular architecture abruptly shows itself off. And graphic representations of architectural plans either depict architecture *sans* people, or architecture surrounded by computer-generated humanoids with all of the 'realism' of 'Second Life' avatars or video-game characters. . . . Perhaps there would be nothing amiss in architecture schools being primarily 'design-driven'—if 'design-driven' meant a method of working that took into account how design *initially* and *ultimately* draws meaning from the play of daily human relationships within spaces that define our lives."

5. Tom Farley and Deborah Cohen (2005) argue that the leading killers of our time have environmental causes—from accidents to chronic illnesses, such as heart disease, lung and breast cancers, diabetes, and stroke.

6. As long as we "remove psyche" from the city, Hillman (1990, 53) warns, "we are unconscious in regard to it" and unable to effectively transform it.

7. For other research findings that exposure to nature can be restorative for children, see Kaplan (2002), Davis (2004), and Kuo and Taylor (2004).

8. Zeynep Toker and Henrik Minassians (2011) also emphasize that "isolated prescriptions for a 'good' urban form and a 'healthy' society oversimplify the interaction between space and society."

9. The *Oxford English Dictionary* defines urbanity as "courtesy, refinement, or elegance of manner," in use since 1825, as well as "life in a city," in use since 1898.

10. Thomas Moore (1992) elaborates on Hillman's recommendation that we learn from the Renaissance doctrine of *anima mundi*, bringing soul back into the world.

11. The Dalai Lama (1990) points out that "taking care of the planet is nothing special, nothing sacred, and nothing holy. It is something like taking care of our own house." Taking care of cities in particular has been described by Roberta Brandes Gratz (1994) as "urban husbandry."

12. See http://groundworkcitybuilding.com/docs/4-energy-district.pdf; http://groundwork citybuilding.com/docs/3-energy-assets.pdf; and http://groundworkcitybuilding.com /docs/2-public-perception.pdf.

Chapter 7. From Good to Great Urbanism: Beyond Sustainability to Prosperity

1. While Maslow recognized that people who are self-actualizing favor "Being-cognition," which focuses on what they have (their own gifts), as opposed to "Deficiency-cognition," which is self-critical, his hierarchy of needs is a model built on the deficiencies.

2. This may be similar to what Donald Schön described as "problem-setting" (Schön 1984).

3. According to Steven Burian, Department of Civil and Environmental Engineering, University of Utah (conversation).

4. Cofounded by Fritjof Capra, Peter Buckley, and Zenobia Barlow in 2005, the Center for EcoLiteracy provides "education for sustainable living [that] cultivates competencies of head, heart, hands, and spirit to enable children to develop toward becoming citizens capable of designing and maintaining sustainable societies" (http://www.ecoliteracy.org). The Society for Organizational Learning was founded in 1997 by Peter Senge (http://www.solonline.org).

5. Led by Ann Forsyth and Joanne Richardson, Design for Health is "a collaborative project that serves to bridge the gap between the emerging research base on community design and healthy living and the everyday realities of local government planning" (Forsyth and Richardson 2011).

6. The mission of Shaping Footprints is "to encourage the regeneration of community and commerce by reshaping how and where we live, learn and work" (Shaping Footprints 2011).

7. The Active Living Research Program was established by the Robert Wood Johnson Foundation, which has supported significant work on the relationship between public health and the built environment.

8. See http://www.design.upenn.edu/city-regional-planning/letter.

Chapter 8. Sideways Urbanism: Rotating the Pyramid

1. The most significant urban visioning of recent years has consisted of efforts to learn from earlier city-building traditions (New Urbanism) along with efforts to achieve sustainable or net-zero cities by applying the most advanced construction, transportation, and communication technologies.

2. In *Urban Design Reclaimed*, Emily Talen (2009) provides step-by-step instructions for anyone interested in advancing an urban design proposal.

3. The Urban Ecology and Design Laboratory (UEDLAB), for example, led by Alex Felson, "works closely with stakeholders and communities through trans- and interdisciplinary collaboration, often combining bottom-up (community engagement, stone soup model) and top-down (design, site planning and experimental research) approaches to reach consensus and generate opportunities for all" (UEDLAB 2011).

4. Instead, Haworth (1965) maintained, they should "find out what people are trying to do, identify the features of the urban environment that stand in the way of their doing those things, and then devise alterations which remove the obstacles." He upheld Jane Jacobs as an exemplar of the latter.

5. Campanella (2011, 15) similarly identifies the goal of planning as "more just, sustainable, healthful, efficient, and beautiful cities and urban regions."

6. Campanella (2011, 15) elaborates:

> In addition to being taught courses in economics and law and governance, students should be trained to be keen observers of the urban landscapes about them, to be able to decipher the riddles of architectural style and substance, to have a working knowledge of the historical development of places and patterns on the land. They should understand how the physical infrastructure of a city works—the mechanics of transportation and utility systems, sewerage and water supply. They should know the fundamentals of ecology and the natural systems of a place, be able to read a site and its landform and vegetation, know that a great spreading maple in the middle of a stand of pines once stood alone in an open pasture. They need to know the basics of impact analysis and be able to assess the implications of a proposed development on traffic, water quality and a city's carbon footprint. And while they cannot master all of site engineering, they should be competent site analysts and—more important—be fluent in assessing the site plans of others. Such training would place competency in the shaping and stewardship of the built environment at the very center of the planning-education solar system.

7. Alex Krieger (2000) identifies nine points that encompass the ideal planner. Among them is the ability to be "situationalists" as opposed to ideologues.

8. Krieger (2009, vii) defines urban design as follows: "Urban design is less a technical discipline and more a mindset among those, of varying disciplinary foundations, seeking, sharing and advocating insights about forms of community. What binds different urban designers are their commitment to city life, the enterprise of urban-maintenance, and the determination to enhance urbanism."

9. A national consortium of more than eighty colleges and universities released a report documenting a significant shift toward "scholarship in public." When the academy considers community engagement irrelevant, this report suggests, it renders itself irrelevant and should thus support public scholarship by rewarding it *as scholarship*, not "community service," in tenure and promotion policies (Cantor and Lavine, 2008).

References

2010 Partners. 2009. "Opening Day and Beyond: Leveraging Our Assets to Create Community Connections." http://groundworkcitybuilding.com/docs/opening_day _and_beyond.pdf.

Alberti, Marina. 2008. *Advances in Urban Ecology: Integrating Humans and Ecological Processes in Urban Ecosystems.* New York: Springer.

Alexander, Christopher, Hajo Neis, Artemis Anninou, and Ingrid King. 1987. *A New Theory of Urban Design.* New York: Oxford University Press.

Allsopp, Philip. 2009. "Challenges for Preserving a Sense of Place and Community." Abstract submitted for consideration to the Seventh Annual Arizona Statewide Historic Preservation Partnership Conference.

Al-Waer, Husam, and Hilson Moran. 2010. "Sustainable Innovation of the Year." Competition submission.

American Society of Landscape Architects (ASLA). 2007. "Analysis and Planning Honor Award." http://www.asla.org/awards/2007/07winners/439_gftuw.html_

Arrien, Angeles. 1993. *The Four-Fold Way.* San Francisco: Harper.

Attoe, Wayne, and Donn Logan. 1989. *American Urban Architecture: Catalysts in the Design of Cities.* Berkeley: University of California Press.

Bachelard, Gaston. 1994. *The Poetics of Space.* Boston: Beacon (1958 original in French).

Barnett, Erica C. 2009. "McGinn, Nickels Campaigns Trade Jabs on Mayor's Enviro Record." *Slog News & Arts.* March 26. Accessed August 28, 2011. http://slog.thestranger .com/slog/archives/2009/03/26/mcginn-nickels-campaigns-trade-jabs-on-mayors -enviro-record.

Barnett, Jonathan. 2011. *City Design: Modernist, Traditional, Green, and Systems Perspectives.* New York: Routledge.

Barth, John. 1986. *Tidewater Tales.* Baltimore, MD: Johns Hopkins University Press.

Beatley, Timothy. 2004. *Native to Nowhere: Sustaining Home and Community in a Global Age.* Washington, DC: Island Press.

Benfield, Kaid. 2011. "Designing Community: Candy Chang's 'Before I Die' Project." *The Atlantic*. May 12. Accessed August 9. http://www.theatlantic.com/life/archive/2011/05 /designing-community-candy-changs-before-i-die-project/238803/.

Benyus, Janine M. 1997. *Biomimicry: Innovation Inspired by Nature*. New York: Perennial.

———. 2010. "Recognizing What Works: A Conscious Emulation of Life's Genius." In *What We See: Advancing the Investigations of Jane Jacobs,* ed. Stephen Goldsmith and Lynne Elizabeth, 194–204. Oakland, CA: New Village.

Berg, Steve. 2008. "New Twins Ballpark Won't Succeed as an Isolated Gem." *Minneapolis Post*. April 22. Accessed August 1, 2011. http://www.minnpost.com/steveberg/ 2008/04 /22/1587/ballpark_wont_succeed_as_an_iso.

Berrizbeitia, Anita, and Linda Pollak. 1999. *Inside Outside: Between Architecture and Landscape*. Gloucester, MA: Rockport.

Best, Alan. 2010. "Utah's Secret." *Planning Magazine*, October, 28–33.

Blaes, Dina. 2010. "Planning Seminar Report." Manuscript.

Block, Peter. 2008. *Community: The Structure of Belonging*. San Francisco: Berrett-Koehler.

Blokland, Talja, and Mike Savage, eds. 2008. *Networked Urbanism: Social Capital in the City*. Farnham, UK: Ashgate.

Brosi, George. 1997. "The Research Paper Thesis." Eastern Kentucky University English Department. Last modified September 25, 1997. Accessed January 2010. http://www.english .eku.edu/services/comp102/hand12.htm.

Burt, Ronald S. 2005. *Brokerage and Closure: An Introduction to Social Capital*. New York: Oxford University Press.

Busquets, Joan, and Felipe Correa, eds. 2007. *Cities X Lines: A New Lens for the Urbanistic Project*. Cambridge, MA: Harvard Graduate School of Design.

Calthorpe, Peter, William Fulton, and Robert Fishman. 2001. *The Regional City: Planning for the End of Sprawl*. Washington, DC: Island Press.

Calvino, Italo. 1978. *Invisible Cities*. New York: Harcourt Brace Jovanovich.

Campanella, Thomas. 2011. "Jane Jacobs and the Death and Life of American Planning." The Design Observer Group. http://places.designobserver.com/feature/jane-jacobs-and -the-death-and-life-of-american-planning/25188/. In *Reconsidering Jane Jacobs*, ed. Max Page and Timothy Mennel. Chicago: American Planning Association, 2011.

Canalscape. 2009a. "Canalscape: AIA Phoenix Metro Chapter Canalscape Competition." http://canalscape.org/activities/aia-phoenix-metro-chapter-canalscape-competition/.

———. 2009b. "Canalscape: Workshop and Studio." http://canalscape.org/activities /workshop-and-studio/.

Cantor, Nancy, and Steven Lavine. 2008. *Scholarship in Public: A Resource on Promotion and Tenure in the Arts, Humanities, and Design*. With Julie Ellison and Timothy K. Eatman. Syracuse, NY: Imagining America, http://imaginingamerica.org/fg-item /scholarship-in-public-knowledge-creation-and-tenure-policy-in-the-engaged -university/.

Chang, Candy. 2009a. "Post-It Notes for Neighbors." Urban Omnibus (website). February 11. http://urbanomnibus.net/2009/02/post-it-notes-for-neighbors/.

———. 2009b. "Street Vendor Guide: Accessible City Regulations." http://candychang .com/street-vendor-guide/.

———. 2011a. "Before I Die: What Is Important to You?" http://candychang.com /before-i-die-in-nola/.

———. 2011b. Interview with Jennifer J. Johnson.

———. 2011c. "I Wish This Was: Civic Input On-Site." http://candychang.com/i-wish -this-was/.

———. 2011d. "Neighbor Doorknob Hanger: Hang and Share Resources." http:// candychang.com/neighbor-doorknob-hanger/.

———. 2011e. "The Stone Cold Facts." http://candychang.com/about/.

Coalition for Utah's Future. 1999. "The History of Envision Utah: A Partnership for Quality Growth." http://www.fta.dot.gov/documents/envision_utah.pdf.

Collective Intelligence Research Institute. 2012. http://ciresearchinstitute.org/. Accessed January 21, 2012.

Condon, Patrick M. 2010. *Seven Rules for Sustainable Communities: Design Strategies for the Post-Carbon World*. Washington, DC: Island Press.

Cooperrider, David L., and Diana Whitney. 2005. *Appreciative Inquiry: A Positive Revolution in Change*. San Francisco: Berrett-Koehler.

Corburn, Jason. 2009. *Toward the Healthy City*. Cambridge, MA: MIT Press.

Corner, James. 1999. "Field Operations." In *Architecture of the Borderlands*, Architectural Design 69, ed. Teddy Cruz and Anne Boddington, 53–55. New York: Wiley.

Crow, Michael. 2007. "American Research Universities during the Long Twilight of the Stone Age." February 21. Manuscript.

Csikszentmihalyi, Mihaly. 1990. *Flow: The Psychology of Optimal Experience*. New York: Harper & Row.

Cullen, Gordon. 1961. *The Concise Townscape*. New York: Reinhold.

Dalai Lama. 1990. "Spirituality and Nature." His Holiness the 14th Dalai Lama of Tibet. September 14. http://www.dalailama.com/messages/environment/spirituality-and -nature.

Dannenberg, Andrew, Howard Frumkin, and Richard Jackson, eds. 2011. *Making Healthy Places: Designing and Building for Health, Well-Being, and Sustainability*. Washington, DC: Island Press.

David, Joshua. 2002. "Reclaiming the High Line: A Project of the Design Trust for Public Space and Friends of the High Line." Edited by Karen Hock. Accessed August 15, 2011. http://www.designtrust.org/pubs/01_Reclaiming_High_Line.pdf.

Davis, John. 2004. "Psychological Benefits of Nature Experiences." Naropa University and School of Lost Borders.

deLaittre, Mary. 2011. Interview with Jennifer J. Johnson.

De Landa, Manuel. 1998. "Extensive Borderlines and Intensive Borderlines." In *BorderLine*, ed. Lebbeus Woods and Ekkehard Rehfeld. New York: Springer.

De Solà-Morales, Manuel. 2004. "The Strategy of Urban Acupuncture." Presented at the Structure Fabric and Topography Conference, Nanjing University, Nanjing, China, May 29–31.

Dunham-Jones, Ellen, and June Williamson. 2008. *Retrofitting Suburbia*. New York: Wiley.

Edwards, Andrés R. 2010. *Thriving beyond Sustainability: Pathways to a Resilient Society*. Gabriola, BC: New Society Publishers, 2010.

Ellin, Nan, ed. 1997. *Architecture of Fear*. New York: Princeton Architectural Press.

———. 2006. *Integral Urbanism*. New York: Routledge.

———. 2008. "Canalscape Could Become Phoenix Legacy." *Arizona Republic*, March 26. http://canalscape.org/press/canalscape-could-become-phoenix-legacy/.

———. 2009. "Canalscape" and "The Tao of Urbanism." In *Canalscape*, ed. Nan Ellin, 3–5 and 46–8. Phoenix: Arizona Board of Regents.

———. 2010a. "The Tao of Urbanism." In *What We See: Advancing the Investigations of Jane Jacobs*, ed. Stephen Goldsmith and Lynne Elizabeth, 44–54. Oakland, CA: New Village Press.

———. 2010b. "Restorative Urbanism: Beyond Sustainability to Prosperity." *Environment & Landscape Architecture of Korea*, December, 142–49.

———. 2012. "Your City, Your Self." In *Imperfect Heath: The Medicalization of Architecture*, 250–66. Montreal: Canadian Centre for Architecture and Lars Müller.

Ellis, Cliff. 2005. "Planning Methods and Good City Form." *Journal of Architectural and Planning Research* 22, no. 2 (Summer): 138–47.

Emmi, Philip. 2010. "Crisis or Climacteric: An Exploration of Trends, Cycles, and Phase Shifts in Human-Environmental Relationships." Presentation.

———. 2011. "A Planning Curriculum for an Era of Transition." Manuscript.

Envision Utah. 2011a. "About Envision Utah: The Envision Utah Process." Accessed July 30. http://www.envisionutah.org/eu_about_euprocess.html and http://www.envisionutah.org/historyenvisonutahv5p1.pdf.

———. 2011b. "Envision Utah: How We Grow Matters." Accessed July 30. http://www.envisionutah.org/index.html.

———. 2011c. "The History of Envision Utah." Accessed July 30. http://www.envisionutah.org/historyenvisonutahv5p1.pdf.

———. 2012. "Brief Overview of Envision Utah."

Erickson, Arthur. 1980. "Shaping." In *The City as Dwelling*, ed. Arthur Erickson, William H. Whyte, and James Hillman. Dallas: Dallas Institute of Humanities and Culture.

ESPN the Magazine. 2010. "Ultimate Standings: 2010." http://espn.go.com/sportsnation/teamrankings/_/year/2010/sport/mlb/category/stx#table.

Ewing, Reid, Susan Handy, Ross Brownson, Otto Clemente, and Emily Winston. 2006. "Identifying and Measuring Urban Design Qualities Related to Walkability." *Journal of Physical Activity & Health* 3, Supp/1: 223–40.

Faga, Barbara. 2006. *Designing Public Consensus.* Hoboken, NJ: Wiley.

Farley, Tom, and Deborah Cohen. 2005. *Prescription for a Healthy Nation: A New Approach to Improving Our Lives by Fixing Our Everyday World.* Boston, MA: Beacon.

Farr, Douglas. 2007. *Sustainable Urbanism: Urban Design with Nature.* Hoboken, NJ: Wiley.

Feldman, Samuel. 2009. "Water Defines Us." Canalscape Workshop.

———. 2011. Interview with Jennifer J. Johnson.

Finn, Robin. 2008. "Two Friends and the Dream of a Lofty Park Realized." *New York Times,* July 8. Accessed July 14, 2011. http://www.nytimes.com/2008/07/11/nyregion/11lives.html.

Florida, Richard. 2009. "How the Crash Will Reshape America." *Atlantic,* March. http://www.theatlantic.com/doc/200903/meltdown-geography/6.

Forester, John F. 1989. *Planning in the Face of Power.* Berkeley: University of California Press.

———. 1999. *The Deliberative Practitioner: Encouraging Participatory Planning Processes.* Cambridge, MA: MIT Press.

Forman, Richard T. T. 1995. *Land Mosaics: The Ecology of Landscapes and Regions.* New York: Cambridge University Press.

Forman, Richard T. T., and Michel Godron. 1986. *Landscape Ecology.* New York: Wiley.

Forsyth, Ann, and Joanne Richardson. 2011. Design for Health (website). Accessed August 1. http://www.designforhealth.net/.

Fournier, Jim. 1999. "Meta-Nature." December 23. http://www.geoman.com/jim/metanature.html.

Frampton, Kenneth. 1999. "Seven Points for the Millennium: An Untimely Manifesto." *Architectural Record,* August, 15.

Friedmann, John. 2000. "The Good City: In Defense of Utopian Thinking." *International Journal of Urban and Regional Research* 24, no. 2: 460–72.

Friends of the High Line. 2005. "Mayor Bloomberg Announces City Acquires High Line from CSX Transportation." Press release (PR Newswire), November 16. Accessed July 24, 2011.

Frumkin, Howard, Lawrence D. Frank, and Richard Jackson. 2004. *Urban Sprawl and Public Health.* Washington, DC: Island Press.

Fukuyama, Francis. 1995. *Trust: The Social Virtues and the Creation of Prosperity.* New York: Free Press.

Geertz, Clifford. 1995. *Local Knowledge: Further Essays in Interpretive Anthropology.* New York: Basic Books.

Gehl, Jan. 2010. *Cities for People.* Washington, DC: Island Press.

———. 2011. *Life between Buildings: Using Public Space*. 6th ed. Washington, DC: Island Press.

Gladwell, Malcolm. 2000. *The Tipping Point*. Boston: Little, Brown.

Glazer, Nathan. 2007. *From a Cause to a Style: Modernist Architecture's Encounter with the American City*. Princeton, NJ: Princeton University Press.

Goldmark, Alex. 2010. "Jim Oberstar Exit Interview after 17 Terms with House Transportation Committee." *Transportation Nation*, December 3. Accessed August 18, 2011. http://transportationnation.org/2010/12/03/ jim-oberstar-exit-interview-after-46 -years-with-house-transportation-committee/.

Governor's Office of Planning and Budget (GOPB). 2000. "Strategy Analysis: QGET– Quality Growth Efficiency Tools." May.

Gratz, Roberta Brandes. 1994. *The Living City: How America's Cities Are Being Revitalized by Thinking Small in a Big Way*. Washington, DC: Preservation Press.

Greenberg, Ken. 2011. *Walking Home: The Life and Lessons of a City Builder*. Toronto: Random House.

Grow, Robert. 2012. Interview with Nan Ellin. March.

Hall, Peter. 2009. "A Good Argument." *Metropolis Magazine*, March.

Hammond, Robert. 2011. Interview with Joshua Edward.

Harries, Karsten. 1998. *The Ethical Function of Architecture*. Cambridge, MA: MIT Press.

Hawken, Paul. 1993. *The Ecology of Commerce: A Declaration of Sustainability*. New York: Harper Business.

———. 2007. *Blessed Unrest: How the Largest Movement in the World Came into Being and Why No One Saw it Coming*. New York: Viking.

Hawken, Paul, Amory Lovins, and Hunter Lovins. 1999. *Natural Capitalism: Creating the Next Industrial Revolution*. New York: Little, Brown.

Haworth, Lawrence. 1965. "The Good City and Urban Design." Paper presented at Ohio Valley Chapter meeting of AIP at Ohio State University, February 26.

Healey, Patsy. 2006. *Collaborative Planning: Shaping Places in Fragmented Societies*. 2nd ed. New York: Palgrave Macmillan.

Heidegger, Martin. 1971. "Building, Dwelling, Thinking." In *Poetry, Language, Thought*, trans. and intro. by Albert Hofstadter. New York: Harper & Row. (Article originally published in 1954.)

Hellmund, Paul, and Daniel S. Smith. 2006. *Designing Greenways: Sustainable Landscapes for Nature and People*. Washington, DC: Island Press.

High Line. 2011. "High Line History." Accessed July 14. http://www.thehighline.org /about/high-line-history.

Hill, Shelby. 2010. "The Canalscape Project Envisions Beautifying Phoenix's Many Canals." *Arizona Business*, December 6. http://aznow.biz/real-estate/canalscape -envisions-beautifying-phoenix-canals.

Hiller, Jennifer. 2011. "Manhattan's Elevated Park Still Reaping Praise for S.A. Native." *San Antonio Express-News.* Updated August 3. Accessed August 15. http://www .mysanantonio.com/life/article/riding-high-1625746.php.

Hillman, James. 1987. "Power and Gemeinschaftsgefuhl." In *City and Soul.* New York: Spring Publications, 2006.

———. 1990. "'Man Is by Nature a Political Animal': Patient as Citizen." In *City and Soul,* 52–53. New York: Spring Publications, 2006.

———. 2006. *City and Soul.* New York: Spring Publications.

———. 2008. Personal communication with author.

———. 2011. "America and the Shift in Ages: An Interview with Jungian James Hillman." Interview with Pythia Peay. *Huffington Post,* February 26. http://www .huffingtonpost.com/pythia-peay/america-and-the-shift-in-_b_822913.html.

Hooper City. 2011. "Welcome to Hooper City." http://hoopercity.com/.

Hough, Michael. 1995. *Cities and Natural Process: A Basis for Sustainability.* New York: Routledge.

Huntsman, Jon, Jr. 2006. *Deseret Morning News,* May 5.

Inam, Aseem. 2011. "Designing Urban Transformation." Boston Society of Architects Lecture Series video, 55:49. April 17. http://www.architects.org/news/aseem-inam -designing-urban-transformation.

Jacobs, Allan B., and Donald Appleyard. 1987. "Toward an Urban Design Manifesto." *Journal of the American Planning Association* 53, no. 1: 112–20.

Jacobs, Jane. 1961. *Death and Life of Great American Cities.* New York: Vintage.

Jackson, Maria Rosario, Florence Kabwasa-Green, and Joaquín Herranz. 2006. "Cultural Vitality in Communities: Interpretation and Indicators." *Urban Institute,* December 11. http://www.urban.org/url.cfm?id=311392.

Jones, Casey. 2011. Interview with Joshua Edward.

Kaplan, Rachel. 2002. "Adolescents and the Natural Environment." In *Children and Nature,* ed. Peter H. Kahn and Stephen R. Kellert, 227–57. Cambridge, MA: MIT Press.

Kay, Braden. 2011. Interview with Jennifer J. Johnson.

Kelbaugh, Doug, ed. 1996. *Pedestrian Pocket Book: A New Suburban Design Strategy.* Princeton, NJ: Princeton Architectural Press.

Kelly, Kevin. 1999. *New Rules for the New Economy.* New York: Penguin.

Kemmis, Daniel. 1995. *The Good City and the Good Life.* New York: Houghton Mifflin.

Kenda, Barbara. 1998. "On the Renaissance Art of Well-Being: Pneuma in Villa Eolia." *RES 34* (Autumn): 101–17.

Keynes, John Maynard. 1963. "Economic Possibilities for our Grandchildren." In *Essays in Persuasion,* 358–73. New York: Norton. (Orig. pub. 1930.)

Kim, W. Chan, and Renée Mauborgne. 2005. *Blue Ocean Strategy: How to Create Uncontested Market Space and Make Competition Irrelevant.* Boston: Harvard Business School Press.

The Knight Foundation. 2011. *Soul of the Community: Why Do We Live Where We Live?* Gallup, and John S. and James L. Knight Foundation. Video. Accessed August 2. http://www.soulofthecommunity.org.

Koh, Jusuck, and Anemone Beck-Koh. 2007. "Landscape Is What; Landscape Is How: A Landscape Approach to Contemporary Urbanism." Presentation at Articulating Landscape Urbanism: A Landscape Approach to Urban Design and Regeneration conference, Wageningen University and Research Center, The Netherlands, May 11–12.

Koolhaas, Rem. 2010. "Advancement versus Apocalypse." In *Ecological Urbanism,* ed. Mohsen Mostafavi and Gareth Doherty, 56–71. Baden: Lars Müller Publishers.

Kretzmann, John, and John McKnight. 1993. *Building Communities from the Inside Out: A Path toward Finding and Mobilizing a Community's Assets.* Chicago: ACTA Publications.

Krieger, Alex. 2000. "The Planner as Urban Designer: Reforming Planning Education." In *The Profession of City Planning: Changes, Images and Challenges: 1950–2000,* ed. Lloyd Rodwin and Bishwapriya Sanyal. New Brunswick, NJ: Center for Urban Policy Research/Rutgers University Press.

———. 2009. "Territories of Urban Design." In *Urban Design,* ed. Alex Krieger and William S. Saunders. Minneapolis: University of Minnesota Press.

Kunstler, James Howard. 1993. *The Geography of Nowhere.* New York: Simon and Schuster.

Kuo, Frances E., and Andrea Faber Taylor. 2004. "A Potential Natural Treatment for Attention-Deficit/Hyperactivity Disorder." *American Journal of Public Health* 94, no. 9 (September): 1580–86.

Landis, John. 2011. "Letter from the Chair of Planning." Accessed August 5. http://www.design.upenn.edu/city-regional-planning/letter.

Landry, Charles. 2000. *The Creative City: A Toolkit for Urban Innovators.* London: Earthscan.

———. 2006. "Lineages of the Creative City," 1–13. http://www.charleslandry.com/index.php?l=articles.

Leadbeater, Charles. 2008. *We-Think: Mass Innovation, Not Mass Production.* London: Profile Books.

Lerner, Jaime. 2003. *Acupunctura Urbana.* Rio de Janeiro: Editora Record.

———. 2010. "Reviving Cities." In *What We See: Advancing the Investigations of Jane Jacobs,* ed. Stephen Goldsmith and Lynne Elizabeth. Oakland, CA: New Village Press.

Lévi-Strauss, Claude. 1955. *Tristes Tropiques.* Paris: Plon.

Louv, Richard. 2005. *Last Child in the Woods: Saving Our Children from Nature-Deficit Disorder.* Chapel Hill, NC: Algonquin.

Lovelock, J. E., and C. E. Giffin. 1969. "Planetary Atmospheres: Compositional and Other Changes Associated with the Presence of Life." *Advances in the Astronautical Sciences* 25:179–93.

Lueck, Thomas. 1999. "Up, but Not Running, on the West Side." *New York Times.* July 25.

Luoni, Stephen. 2011. Interview with Jennifer J. Johnson.

Lydon, Mike, Dan Bartman, Ronald Woudstra, and Aurash Khawarzad. 2011. *Tactical Urbanism.* http://patterncities.com/archives/175.

MacEachern, Doug. 2009. "The Valley's Untapped Canals: For a Visionary Group of Land-Use Experts and Historians, It's Time Residents Stopped Turning Their Backs on the Valley's Canals." *Arizona Republic,* July 12. http://www.azcentral.com/arizona republic/viewpoints/articles/2009/07/11/20090711maceachern12-vip.html.

McDonough, William. 2011. "McDonough Stories." April 1. http://www.youtube.com /McDonoughC2C#p/a/u/2/olt-KpyiSzg.

McDonough, William, and Michael Braungart. 2002. *Cradle to Cradle: Remaking the Way We Make Things.* New York: North Point Press.

_____. 2003. *From Principles to Practice: Creating a Sustainable Architecture for the 21st Century.* http://www.mcdonough.com/writings/from_principles.htm.

McGeehan, Patrick. 2011. "The High Line Isn't Just a Site To See; It's Also an Economic Dynamo." June 5. *New York Times.* Accessed August 14. http://www.nytimes .com/2011/06/06/nyregion/with-next-phase-ready-area-around-high-line-is-flourishing .html.

McGehee, Overton. 2005. "Background: Habitat for Humanity." Accessed March 25, 2012. http://www.urban-habitats.org/.

McHarg, Ian. 1969. *Design with Nature.* Garden City, NY: Natural History Press.

McKibben, Bill. 2007. *Deep Economy: The Wealth of Communities and the Durable Future.* New York: Macmillan.

McKnight, John, and Peter Block. 2010. *The Abundant Community.* San Francisco: Berrett-Koehler.

McLaughlin, Peter. 2011. Interview with Jennifer J. Johnson.

Menconi, Lilia. 2009. "Canalscape Opens Tomorrow at ASU." *Phoenix New Times* (Arty Girl), November 9. http://blogs.phoenixnewtimes.com/uponsun/2009/11/arty_girl _canalscape_opens_tom.php.

MLB.com. 2010. "Twins' Target Field Gets Highest LEED Rating of Any Ballpark in America." MLB Advanced Media, L.P. Accessed August 17, 2011. http://mlb.mlb.com /news/article.jsp?ymd=20100408&content_id=9141798&vkey=news_mlb&fext=.jsp&c _id=mlb.

Moore, Thomas. 1992. *Care of the Soul.* New York: HarperCollins.

Morrish, William R. 2011. Interview with Jennifer J. Johnson.

Morrish, William R., and Catherine Brown. 1993. "Infrastructure for the New Social Covenant." In *Writing Urbanism: A Design Reader,* ed. Doug Kelbaugh and Kit Krankel McCullough. New York: Routledge, 2008. (Orig. pub. 1993.)

Morrish, William R., Susanne Schindler, and Katie Swenson. 2009. *Growing Urban Habitats: Seeking New Housing Development Model.* San Francisco: William Stout.

Mostafavi, Mohsen. 2010. "Why Ecological Urbanism? Why Now?" *Harvard Design Magazine,* 32, 1–12.

Mulady, Kathy. 2003. "City Celebrates Park Pioneer Olmsted." April 1. *Seattle Post-Intelligencer.* Accessed August 27, 2011. http://www.seattlepi.com/news/article/City -celebrates-park-pioneer-Olmsted-1111178.php.

Mumford, Lewis. 1937. "What Is a City?" *Architectural Record* 82, no. 5 (November): 59–62.

———. 1938. *The Culture of Cities.* New York: Harcourt, Brace, 1938.

———. 1967–70. *Myth of the Machine.* New York: Harcourt, Brace.

Municipal Arts Society Planning Center. 2011. *Planning for All New Yorkers: A 21st Century Upgrade for New York's Planning Process Based on Recommendations of the Community-Based Planning Task Force.* January. New York: Municipal Arts Society.

National Public Radio (NPR). 2011. "The Inside Track on New York City's High Line." September 3. http://www.northcountrypublicradio.com/news/npr/140063103/the -inside-track-on-new-york-city-s-high-line.

Nelson, G. Lynn. 2004. *Writing and Being.* Novato, CA: New World Library.

Norberg-Schulz, Christian. 1980. *Genius Loci: Towards a Phenomenology of Architecture.* New York: Rizzoli.

Nordström, Kjell, and Jonas Ridderstråle. 1999. *Funky Business: Talent Makes Capital Dance.* London: Pearson Education.

Oldenburg, Ray. 2007. "The Character of Third Places." In *Urban Design Reader,* ed. Matthew Carmona and Steve Tiesdell, 163–69. Boston, MA: Architectural Press. Originally published in *The Great Good Place: Cafés, Coffee Shops, Bookstores, Bars, Hair Salons, and the Other Great Hangouts at the Heart of a Community,* 2nd ed. (Cambridge, MA: Da Capo, 1999).

Onuma, Kimon. 2010. *Get Real with BIM.* Onuma Inc. video. 6:58. November 12. http:// onuma.com/video/ko.html.

———. 2011. Interview with Justinian Popa.

Open Space Seattle. 2011a. "Green Infrastructure Plan: 2100." Accessed August 4. http:// depts.washington.edu/open2100/pdf/openspace_2100.pdf.

———. 2011b. "What Is Open Space Seattle 2100?" http://open2100.org/.

Pogrebin, Robin. 2011. "High Line: The Sequel." *New York Times,* May 28. Accessed August 15. http://www.nytimes.com/2011/05/29/nyregion/coming-soon-to-the-high -line-more-room-to-roam.html.

Project for Public Spaces (PPS). 2004. "Open Letter to the *New York Times.*" *Placemaking* (PPS newsletter), July.

Putnam, Robert. 2000. *Bowling Alone: The Collapse and Revival of American Community*. New York: Simon and Schuster.

Ratti, Carlo, and Anthony Townsend. 2011. "The Social Nexus." *Scientific American*, September, 42–48.

ReGenesis and Taller 13. 2009. "Centro de Arte y Ecologia en Valle de Bravo." July 24. http://issuu.com/taller13/docs/valle_de_bravo__anexos.

Register, Richard. 2006. *Ecocities: Building Cities in Balance with Nature*. Rev. ed. Gabriola, BC: New Society Publishers.

Rosensweig, Dan. 2012. Interview with Nan Ellin. April 12.

Ross, Andrew. 2011. *Bird on Fire: Lessons from the World's Least Sustainable City*. New York: Oxford University Press.

Rottle, Nancy. 2011a. E-mail to author.

———. 2011b. Interview with Jennifer J. Johnson.

Rowe, Peter. 1992. *Making of a Middle Landscape*. Cambridge, MA: MIT Press.

Rudy Bruner Foundation. 2011. http://www.brunerfoundation.org/.

Sandercock, Leonie. 2003. *Cosmopolis II: Mongrel Cities in the 21st Century*. New York: Continuum.

Scearce, Diana. 2011. "Connected Citizens: The Power, Peril, and Potential of Networks." Knight Foundation and Monitor Institute. https://knight.box.net/shared/ng70lqn9hb.

Scharmer, C. Otto. 2007. *Theory U: Leading from the Future as It Emerges*. Cambridge, MA: Society for Organizational Learning.

———. 2010. "The Blind Spot of Institutional Leadership: How to Create Deep Innovation through Moving from Egosystem to Ecosystem Awareness." Paper prepared for World Economic Forum Annual Meeting of the New Champion. Tianjin, People's Republic of China, September 13–15. http://www.ottoscharmer.com/docs/articles/2010_DeepInnovation_Tianjin.pdf.

Scheer, Brenda Case. 2010. *The Evolution of Urban Form*. Chicago: American Planning Association.

Schön, Donald. 1984. *The Reflective Practitioner*. New York: Basic Books.

Schumacher, Lawrence. 2011. "More Garbage-Burning Ahead for Minneapolis?" *Twin Cities Daily Planet*, August 2. Accessed August 19. http://www.tcdailyplanet.net/news/2011/08/02/more-garbage-burning-ahead-minneapolis.

Shakespeare, William. 1590–96. *A Midsummer Night's Dream*.

Shaping Footprints. 2011. http://www.sfpinc.org.

Spretnak, Charlene. 1997. *The Resurgence of the Real: Body, Nature and Place in a Hypermodern World*. New York: Addison-Wesley.

Sprunt, David. 2009. "View from Elsewhere: Impressions of the Grand Canal." Canalscape Studio.

Stavros, Jacqueline, and Gina Hinrichs. 2009. *The Thin Book of SOAR: Building Strengths-Based Strategy*. Bend, OR: Thin Book Publishing.

Sundius, Bo, and Hisako Ichiki. 2011. "Bunch for Tree People." Manuscript.

Swaner, Sumner. 2011. Interview with Jennifer J. Johnson.

Swenson, Katie. 2011. Interview with Jennifer J. Johnson.

Talen, Emily. 2009. *Urban Design Reclaimed*. Chicago: American Planning Association.

Taylor, Kate. 2010. "After High Line's Success, Other Cities Look Up." *New York Times*. July 14. Accessed August 1, 2011. http://www.nytimes.com/2010/07/15/arts /design/15highline.html.

Tetreault, Colin. 2012. E-mail to author. March 7.

Thompson, George F., and Frederick Steiner, eds. 1997. *Ecological Design and Planning*. New York: Wiley.

Todd, Nancy, Jack Todd, and John Todd. 1994. *From Eco-Cities to Living Machines*. Berkeley, CA: North Atlantic, 1994.

Toker, Zeynep, and Henrik Minassians. 2011. "Good Cities and Healthy Communities for a Better Quality of Life." Abstract, ACSP Conference, Salt Lake City, Utah.

Tuan, Yi-Fu. 1990. *Topophilia: A Study of Environmental Perception, Attitudes, and Values*. New York: Columbia University, 1990. (Orig. pub. 1974 by Prentice Hall.)

Tzonis, Alexander, and Liane Lefaivre. 1999. "Beyond Monuments, Beyond Zip-a-thon." *Le Carré Bleu* (3–4): 4–44.

United Nations. 1987. *Our Common Future: Brundtland Report*. UN World Commission on Environment and Development. August 4.

University of Arkansas Community Design Center (UACDC). 2009. "Porchscapes: Between Neighborhood Watershed and Home." http://uacdc.uark.edu/books /excerpts/18Porchscapes.pdf.

———. 2011a. *Low-Impact Development: A Design Manual for Urban Areas*. http://uacdc .uark.edu/pop_book.php?bid=26.

———. 2011b. "Vision." http://uacdc.uark.edu/contact.php.

University of Arkansas Newswire. 2011. "Design Manual for Low-Impact Development Garners Second National Award: Book Wins ASLA Award of Excellence in Communications." September 28. http://newswire.uark.edu/Article.aspx?ID=16864.

Urban Ecology and Design Laboratory (UEDLAB). 2011. "About UEDLAB." http:// uedlab.org/about. Accessed December 11.

Viljoen, Andre, ed. 2005. *Continuous Productive Urban Landscapes*. Oxford: Architectural Press.

Wakefield, Roger. 2007. "What Is Autism?" *Ian & Lynn Langtree's Disabled World*. October 30. Accessed September 5, 2011. http://www.disabled-world.com/.

Waldheim, Charles. 2006. *Landscape Urbanism*. New York: Princeton Architectural Press.

Weinstein, Norman. 2009a. "Words That Build: Offer an Opening Statement That Frames a Broad Vista." *ArchNewsNow.com*. November 3, 2009. http://www.archnewsnow .com/features/Feature312.htm.

———. 2009b. "Words That Build: Work with Clients to Develop Plans That Place Human/Spatial Relationships First." *ArchNewsNow.com*. August 4. http://www .archnewsnow.com/features/Feature302.htm.

Welch, Craig. 2010. "Seattle Mayor Greg Nickels' Green Agenda Wasn't Enough." *Seattle Times*, January 16. Accessed August 28, 2011. http://seattletimes.nwsource.com/html /pacificnw/2010724154_pacificpgonickels17.html.

Wexler, Mark. 1998. "Money Does Grow on Trees—and So Does Better Health and Happiness." *National Wildlife*, April–May, 70.

Index